1st Workshop on Customized Chat Grounding Persona and Knowledge

Held at COLING 2022

Gyeongju, South Korea
12 – 17 October 2022

ISBN: 978-1-7138-6147-8

Printed from e-media with permission by:

Curran Associates, Inc.
57 Morehouse Lane
Red Hook, NY 12571

Some format issues inherent in the e-media version may also appear in this print version.

Printed with permission by Curran Associates, Inc. (2023)

For permission requests, please contact the Association for Computational Linguistics
at the address below.

Association for Computational Linguistics
209 N. Eighth Street
Stroudsburg, Pennsylvania 18360

Phone: 1-570-476-8006
Fax: 1-570-476-0860

acl@aclweb.org

Additional copies of this publication are available from:

Curran Associates, Inc.
57 Morehouse Lane
Red Hook, NY 12571 USA
Phone: 845-758-0400
Fax: 845-758-2633
Email: curran@proceedings.com
Web: www.proceedings.com

COLING

International Conference on Computational Linguistics

Proceedings of the Conference and Workshops

COLING

Volume 29 (2022), No. 13

Proceedings of 1st Workshop on Customized Chat Grounding Persona and Knowledge

The 29th International Conference on Computational Linguistics

October 12 - 17, 2022
Gyeongju, Republic of Korea

ISSN 2951-2093

Preface

It is our great pleasure to welcome you to the 1st Workshop on Customized Chat Grounding Persona and Knowledge, which is held in Gyeongju, Korea on October 16, 2022, in conjunction with the 29th International Conference on Computational Linguistics (COLING 2022).

The workshop aims to provide a forum for researchers who share their prospects and latest discoveries on a customized conversational model. Humans usually have conversations by making use of prior knowledge about a topic and background information of the people to whom they are talking. However, existing conversational agents and datasets do not consider such comprehensive information, and thus they have a limitation in generating utterances where the knowledge and persona are fused properly. Following the manner of human conversation, a conversational agent's ability to have a conversation with customized answers from prior knowledge and user's personal information is crucial for satisfying the users. In the workshop, we hope that next-generation conversational agents would be discussed, which are capable of choosing the proper persona and knowledge to answer the question from the users, and generating more knowledgeable and customized answers, reflecting both knowledge and persona.

In this year, 7 technical papers with 2 full papers and 5 short papers were submitted from various institutions in 4 countries. Each paper was reviewed by at least two committees among 4 primary program committees and 16 program committees. After the reviewing process, 2 full papers and 4 short papers have finally been accepted, and 2 full papers and 2 short papers are included in the proceedings. The authors of all accepted papers will present their work orally and have QA session. Following the reviews, two outstanding papers are nominated as the best papers of our workshop, the papers of Selene Baez Santamaria et al. and Young-Jun Lee et al.

Moreover, we are delighted to invite Mikhail Burtsev (researcher at AIRI and DeepPavlov.ai), Youngbum Kim (researcher at Naver Search US), and Jaegul Choo (professor at KAIST) as keynote speakers. The final program is announced on the official workshop website: https://sites.google.com/view/persona-knowledge-workshop.

We look forward to welcoming you all at the 1st workshop on customized chat grounding persona and knowledge!

Heuiseok Lim, Seungryong Kim, Yeonsoo Lee, Steve Lin, Paul Hongsuck Seo, and Yumin Suh

Organizers

Heuiseok Lim, Korea University, Republic of Korea
Seungryong Kim, Korea University, Republic of Korea
Yeonsoo Lee, Language AI Lab, NCSOFT, Republic of Korea
Steve Lin, Microsoft Research Asia, China
Paul Hongsuck Seo, Google Research
Yumin Suh, NEC Labs, USA

Primary Program Committees

Yoonna Jang, Ph.D. student, Korea University, Republic of Korea
Jungwoo Lim, Ph.D. student, Korea University, Republic of Korea
Yuna Hur, Ph.D. student, Korea University, Republic of Korea
Suhyune Son, Ph.D. student, Korea University, Republic of Korea

Program Committees

Hyeoncheol Kim, Korea University, Republic of Korea
Youngjoong Ko, Sungkyunkwan University, Republic of Korea
Harksoo Kim, Konkuk University, Republic of Korea
Jaehoon Cha, Science and Technology Facilities Council, UK
Weifeng SU, UIC, China
Jaechoon Cho, Hanshin University, Republic of Korea
Yeongwook Yang, Hanshin University, Republic of Korea
Yeochan Yoon, Jeju National University, Republic of Korea
Aiyanyo Imatitikua Danielle, Human-inspired AI Research, Republic of Korea
Jaehyun Park, Language AI Lab. NCSOFT, Republic of Korea
Hyesung Ji, Language AI Lab. NCSOFT, Republic of Korea
Youngrok Cha, Language AI Lab., NCSOFT, Republic of Korea
Sangha Nam, Language AI Lab., NCSOFT, Republic of Korea
Moonsu Han, Language AI Lab., NCSOFT, Republic of Korea
Seolhwa Lee, CoAStaL NLP group, University of Copenhagen, Denmark
Chanhee Lee, Naver Search US, US

Sponsors

The 1st Workshop on Customized Chat Grounding Persona and Knowledge is organized with the support of Google (https://about.google/), NCSOFT (https://kr.ncsoft.com/kr/index.do), and ICT Creative Consilience Foundation of Korea University.

Keynote Speakers

Mikhail Burtsev, AIRI / DeepPavlov.ai
YoungBum Kim, Naver Search US
Jaegul Choo, KAIST

Table of Contents

Focus on FoCus: Is FoCus focused on Context, Knowledge and Persona?

SeungYoon Lee[1†], Jungseob Lee[2†], Chanjun Park[2,3], Sugyeong Eo[2], Hyeonseok Moon[2], Jaehyung Seo[2], Jeongbae Park[4*], Heuiseok Lim[2,4*]
[1]Chung-Ang University, [2]Korea University, [3]Upstage,
[4]Human Inspired Artificial Intelligence Research (HIAI)
dltmddbs100@cau.ac.kr, chanjun.park@upstage.ai
{omanma1928,bcj1210,djtnrud,glee889,seojae777,insmile,limhseok}@korea.ac.kr

Abstract

Rather than continuing the conversation based on personalized or implicit information, the existing conversation system generates dialogue by focusing only on the superficial content. To solve this problem, FoCus was recently released (Jang et al., 2022). FoCus is a persona-knowledge grounded dialogue generation dataset that leverages Wikipedia's knowledge and personal persona, focusing on the landmarks provided by Google, enabling user-centered conversation. However, a closer empirical study is needed since research in the field is still in its early stages. Therefore, we fling two research questions about FoCus. (i) *"Is the FoCus whether for conversation or question answering?"* to identify the structural problems of the dataset. (ii) *"Does the FoCus model do real knowledge blending?"* to closely demonstrate that the model acquires actual knowledge. As a result of the experiment, we present that the FoCus model could not correctly blend the knowledge according to the input dialogue and that the dataset design is unsuitable for the multi-turn conversation.

1 Introduction

Recent studies have widely considered knowledge grounded dialogue, user interest, and preference (Dinan et al., 2018; Zhou et al., 2018a; Zhang et al., 2019; Zhao et al., 2020; Zheng et al., 2020; Meng et al., 2020; Song et al., 2021; Majumder et al., 2021; Galetzka et al., 2021). Especially, Zhang et al. (2018) presented persona-chat dataset based on personalizing dialogue agents. Similarly, Rashkin et al. (2018) constructed conversation dataset with emotional labels according to the given situation. In different way, Dinan et al. (2018) and Zhou et al. (2018b) focused on generating dialogue based on knowledge retrieved from Wikipedia.

However, those existing dialogue datasets do not comprehensively consider the user persona of the given situation and knowledge of the grounded object. The biased dataset toward persona or knowledge quickly undermines the user's intention or purpose, and rendering high-quality answers is challenging. From this point of view, dialogue generation through the proper blending of persona and knowledge is a significant issue that should be considered in advanced research. To fulfill this purpose, Jang et al. (2022) has released FoCus and baseline models based on the grounded persona and knowledge.

To the best of our knowledge, FoCus is the first persona-knowledge grounded dialogue dataset that incorporates knowledge and customized persona. However, related research in the persona-knowledge is still insufficient, and Jang et al. (2022) only provides descriptions of the dataset and has not corroborated the weakness of the dataset and model architecture. Furthermore, no in-depth analysis has been conducted on whether the model engages in conversation based on the blended persona-knowledge.

To demonstrate these problems, we intend to conduct an in-depth analysis of the proposed model and dataset through an empirical study. In this paper, we execute probing tests by throwing research questions in terms of data-centric (Park et al., 2021; Seo et al., 2022) and model-centric (Park et al., 2020) in the Jang et al. (2022). First, we point out that FoCus is more of a question-answering than a multi-turn dialogue task, under the question *"Is the FoCus whether for conversation or question answering?"* Generally, a multi-turn dialogue dataset forms a context in which two or more speakers continue to conversation. Moreover, the memorable context significantly impacts the generation of the next utterance.

However, we experimentally found that the previous conversation on the FoCus had little effect on

* Corresponding Authors

Proceedings of the 29th International Conference on Computational Linguistic, pages 1–8
October 12–17, 2022.

the next utterance. This is because each round consists of an independent set that is not involved in the context. Therefore, we demonstrate that the FoCus is more of a question-answering task rather than a consistent multi-turn conversation. To closely analyze this point, we conduct a case study according to the change in the conversation order and the inclusion of dialogue histories corresponding to the previous utterance.

Second, we ask, *"Does the FoCus model do real knowledge blending?"* and examine whether the baseline model presented in Jang et al. (2022) is blending properly with persona in selecting the appropriate knowledge for conversation. In this experiment, we proceed with various analyses using BM25 (Robertson et al., 1995), DPR (Karpukhin et al., 2020), STS (Reimers and Gurevych, 2019), and TF-IDF (Salton and Buckley, 1988) as a retrieval module. We analyze performance changes according to the knowledge selection of each search module. Based on this, we attempt to probe what problems the method of blending history and selected knowledge in an in-context approach causes in knowledge grounding.

2 FoCus

2.1 Dataset

FoCus presented by Jang et al. (2022) is a multi-turn dialogue dataset constructed on the landmark content provided by Google Landmarks Dataset v2 (GLDv2) (Weyand et al., 2020), enabling personalized conversation with relevant knowledge and various user personas. The purpose of this dataset is to take user utterances and generate responses leveraging landmark knowledge and an appropriate persona. FoCus comprises human-to-machine conversations, user persona, Wikipedia knowledge, and knowledge candidates. We report the detailed statistics and examples of the dataset in Appendix A.

2.2 Model

The baseline model in the Jang et al. (2022) consists of two steps: a retrieval module and a dialogue module. First, the TF-IDF score-based retrieving algorithm receives the user's utterance and chooses the top-5 knowledge to be transferred to the dialogue module. Next, the dialogue module takes input from the user's persona, selected knowledge and utterances through a learnable Transformer (Vaswani et al., 2017) and pre-trained language models such as GPT-2 (Radford et al., 2019), BART (Lewis et al., 2019). In this process, a subtask called knowledge grounding (KG) and persona grounding (PG) is performed. Based on the selected knowledge and utterance, KG determines the knowledge answer that matches the user utterance among the 10 knowledge candidates presented for each round. Instead of retrieving, PG adopts the persona answer that is consistent with the user utterance among the five persona candidates. The model receives the selected persona and knowledge vector, creating an utterance by blending them. An overview of the model is depicted in Appendix B.

3 Experiments

3.1 Experimental Design

We utilize the same train and validation set with FoCus (Jang et al., 2022) for objective verification. Experiments are implemented based on the baseline models released by the original research[1], the BART-base is adopted for our experiments. All hyper-parameters, including seeds, are run under the same settings, except for exceptional cases marked separately. We fine-tune the model using a single RTX-8000 GPU.

Research Question 01 In order to prove that FoCus is similar to QA composed of independent question-answering pair, we randomly shuffle the order of each round composed of user and model utterances, and then compare the generation score with the original order.

In this setting, the input utterance is mixed for each pair and cuts off the contextual flow according to the round. In addition, this data setting increases randomness because more history is considered during training as the history size increases, which means how far the model can consider past utterances. In accessing the model performance, we adopt the chrF++ (Popović, 2015) score, SacreBLEU (Post, 2018), and ROUGE (Lin, 2004) score for evaluation metrics and compare the average values. In this case, we also consider the history of the conversation during the evaluation.

Research Question 02 We analyze the role of retrieval module in knowledge blending. In the existing baseline, Wikipedia knowledge is included in the conversation through TF-IDF. We additionally use BM25, DPR, and STS to select knowledge and measure grounding performance to check whether

[1]`https://github.com/pkchat-focus/FoCus`

Models	Generation					Average
	chrF++	BLEU	R-1	R-2	R-L	
BART + history = 2	0.2941	11.61	36.84	19.87	32.43	20.21
BART + history = 3	0.2983	12.01	37.19	20.31	32.78	20.52
BART + history = 4	0.2988	12.04	37.37	20.41	32.97	20.62
BART + shuffle + history = 2	0.2991	11.93	37.15	19.98	32.72	20.42
BART + shuffle + history = 3	0.2950	11.96	36.94	19.98	32.63	20.36
BART + shuffle + history = 4	0.2982	11.87	37.12	20.06	32.56	20.38

Table 1: Generation score of validation set under the same experimental environment as FoCus. History refers to how many past conversations are included in model training and evaluation. We randomly shuffle rounds of dialogue and compare them to their original order.

Retrieval	Grounding (Acc.)	
	Persona	Knowledge
TF-IDF	67.43	70.1
BM25	67.43	70.1
DPR	67.43	70.1
STS	67.43	70.1

Table 2: Knowledge and persona grounding performances from four different retrieval modules.

the selected knowledge is normally reflected according to different types of retrieval. We use accuracy as an evaluation metric for KG and PG tasks.

3.2 Is the FoCus whether for conversation or question answering? (Data-Centric)

The experimental results are shown in Table 1. If the dataset has the contextual multi-turn for the utterances flow, the order of previous utterances provides essential information for contextual understanding. However, when comparing the results of randomly shuffling the dialogue turns with the baseline results, there is no significant difference in the model's performance even if the turn of dialogue order is arbitrarily mixed.

As the history size increases, the average of the generation score increases from 20.21 to 20.62, as shown top of Table 1. However, when random shuffling is applied, the largest difference is insignificant at 0.24 (bottom of Table 1) compared to the same history size as random shuffling is not applied. Even when the history size is 2, which is the case of learning only the previous conversation, the score of the shuffled case is higher by 0.21. In general, a long input size leads to an increase in noise as well. Considering this, since we compare under the same conditions within the same history size, the difference in performance cannot be attributed to noise.

Generation scores in random order are similar to correct order, although FoCus has a multi-turn configuration. This result indicates that the dataset is more of a QA rather than a context-influenced conversation.

3.3 Does the FoCus model do real knowledge blending? (Model-Centric)

Table 2 shows the evaluation results on four different retrieval modules. First, as a result of quantitative analysis, even when four different modules are applied, PG accuracy is 67.43 and KG accuracy is 70.1, which is the same for all four modules. Second, we proceed with the qualitative evaluation results for knowledge extraction, and we are able to confirm that each module extracts different knowledge (The top-5 knowledge analysis results extracted by each module are described in Appendix C).

Combining and interpreting the two results, each module shows the same grounding accuracy despite selecting different knowledge. This is presumed to be caused by improper blending in the process of training the knowledge extracted by the model. The knowledge vector extracted from retrieval used in training is quite small compared to the size of persona and history vector to be concatenated. Therefore, it appears that there is relatively little effect on KG.

3.4 Additional Analysis

Ablation study for max-length As a result of comparing the generated sentences with the gold labels in the experimental process for the data-centric approach, we find that the max-length among the hyper-parameters during generation is presented too low. Since the generated sentence is forcibly

max-length	Generation				
	chrF++	BLEU	R-1	R-2	R-L
20 (baseline)	0.2821	10.74	34.84	18.55	30.6
50	0.3259	13.48	37.96	20.66	33.11
75	0.3259	**14.23**	**38.69**	**21.35**	**33.79**
100	**0.3322**	13.98	38.26	20.94	33.41

Table 3: Generation scores according to the extension of max-length.

Models	Generation					Average
	chrF++	BLEU	R-1	R-2	R-L	
BART + history = 2	0.3439	14.44	39.31	21.53	34.11	21.95
BART + history = 3	0.3565	13.86	39.3	21.26	33.49	21.65
BART + history = 4	0.3553	15.47	40.5	22.74	35.3	22.87
BART + history = 6	0.3563	15.17	40.32	22.34	34.9	22.62
BART + shuffle + history = 2	0.3604	14.73	39.39	21.67	33.79	21.99
BART + shuffle + history = 3	0.3455	15.24	39.85	22.36	35	22.56
BART + shuffle + history = 4	0.357	14.33	39.25	21.74	33.62	21.86
BART + shuffle + history = 6	0.3419	14.69	39.44	21.94	34.43	22.17

Table 4: Distribution of generation scores when history size is increased to 6 and max-length to 75. We adjust the history size and max-length to re-run the evaluation. All the other experimental settings are the same.

cut in the middle, it cannot contain as much contextual information as the expressive power of the model. This leads to negative effect on the point we attempt to experiment with, so we compare the parameters by giving them various values in a wider range.

We manually set the max-length to 50, 75, and 100, respectively, and re-evaluate. The experimental results are shown in Table 3. According to the Table 3, the adjustment of the max-length leads to a large improvement in the generation score. In particular, when max-length is set to 75, all scores except chrF++ are the highest. In other words, the existing max-length limits the performance of the model, which means that the model doesn't sufficiently capture the context of the conversation.

Expanding history size with max-length As the history size increases, which indicates the range of consideration of past utterances, the randomness also increases when the round is shuffled, making it more difficult to preserve the context information. Therefore, if the conversation has an element of connectivity, it can cause a significant drop in performance. To observe this more closely, we adjust the max-length to 75 under the same settings as in the previous experiments and conduct a case study by adding the case where the history size is 6. The results are shown in Table 4.

Similarly, the difference in average generation score between the two conditions is not significant in Table 4. Even if the history size is 2 or 3, the randomly mixed case has a higher score. In particular, in the case of shuffled history = 3, some scores are equal to or higher than that of unmixed history = 6. In addition, although the history size is increased to 6, there is a little performance difference between the shuffled case and the non-shuffled case.

This is because each round of the dataset is composed of an independent QA style, so even if the order of information is randomly reversed, it can be interpreted that the model concentrates only on the utterance of the user corresponding to the present and historical information is rarely used. This suggests that FoCus is difficult to be seen as a multi-turn dialogue dataset, and that more contextual information should be considered to construct close to practical dialogue.

4 Conclusion

In this work, we conduct an in-depth analysis of FoCus, which aims to blend knowledge and persona. Experimental results quantitatively demonstrate that the proposed content as a multi-turn dialogue is close to QA and that the model does not appropriately incorporate knowledge to persona. In the future, we plan to properly combine knowledge and persona based on the limitations we presented.

Acknowledgements

This research was supported by Basic Science Research Program through the National Research Foundation of Korea(NRF) funded by the Ministry of Education(NRF-2021R1A6A1A03045425) and MSIT(Ministry of Science and ICT), Korea, under the ITRC(Information Technology Research Center) support program(IITP-2022-2018-0-01405) supervised by the IITP(Institute for Information & Communications Technology Planning Evaluation).

References

Emily Dinan, Stephen Roller, Kurt Shuster, Angela Fan, Michael Auli, and Jason Weston. 2018. Wizard of wikipedia: Knowledge-powered conversational agents. *arXiv preprint arXiv:1811.01241*.

Fabian Galetzka, Jewgeni Rose, David Schlangen, and Jens Lehmann. 2021. Space efficient context encoding for non-task-oriented dialogue generation with graph attention transformer. In *Proceedings of the 59th Annual Meeting of the Association for Computational Linguistics and the 11th International Joint Conference on Natural Language Processing (Volume 1: Long Papers)*, pages 7028–7041.

Yoonna Jang, Jungwoo Lim, Yuna Hur, Dongsuk Oh, Suhyune Son, Yeonsoo Lee, Donghoon Shin, Seungryong Kim, and Heuiseok Lim. 2022. Call for customized conversation: Customized conversation grounding persona and knowledge. In *Proceedings of the AAAI Conference on Artificial Intelligence*, volume 36, pages 10803–10812.

Vladimir Karpukhin, Barlas Oğuz, Sewon Min, Patrick Lewis, Ledell Wu, Sergey Edunov, Danqi Chen, and Wen-tau Yih. 2020. Dense passage retrieval for open-domain question answering. *arXiv preprint arXiv:2004.04906*.

Mike Lewis, Yinhan Liu, Naman Goyal, Marjan Ghazvininejad, Abdelrahman Mohamed, Omer Levy, Ves Stoyanov, and Luke Zettlemoyer. 2019. Bart: Denoising sequence-to-sequence pre-training for natural language generation, translation, and comprehension. *arXiv preprint arXiv:1910.13461*.

Chin-Yew Lin. 2004. Rouge: A package for automatic evaluation of summaries. In *Text summarization branches out*, pages 74–81.

Bodhisattwa Prasad Majumder, Taylor Berg-Kirkpatrick, Julian McAuley, and Harsh Jhamtani. 2021. Unsupervised enrichment of persona-grounded dialog with background stories. *arXiv preprint arXiv:2106.08364*.

Chuan Meng, Pengjie Ren, Zhumin Chen, Weiwei Sun, Zhaochun Ren, Zhaopeng Tu, and Maarten de Rijke. 2020. Dukenet: A dual knowledge interaction network for knowledge-grounded conversation. In *Proceedings of the 43rd International ACM SIGIR Conference on Research and Development in Information Retrieval*, pages 1151–1160.

Chanjun Park, Jaehyung Seo, Seolhwa Lee, Chanhee Lee, Hyeonseok Moon, Sugyeong Eo, and Heui-Seok Lim. 2021. Bts: Back transcription for speech-to-text post-processor using text-to-speech-to-text. In *Proceedings of the 8th Workshop on Asian Translation (WAT2021)*, pages 106–116.

Chanjun Park, Yeongwook Yang, Kinam Park, and Heuiseok Lim. 2020. Decoding strategies for improving low-resource machine translation. *Electronics*, 9(10):1562.

Maja Popović. 2015. chrf: character n-gram f-score for automatic mt evaluation. In *Proceedings of the Tenth Workshop on Statistical Machine Translation*, pages 392–395.

Matt Post. 2018. A call for clarity in reporting bleu scores. *arXiv preprint arXiv:1804.08771*.

Alec Radford, Jeffrey Wu, Rewon Child, David Luan, Dario Amodei, Ilya Sutskever, et al. 2019. Language models are unsupervised multitask learners. *OpenAI blog*, 1(8):9.

Hannah Rashkin, Eric Michael Smith, Margaret Li, and Y-Lan Boureau. 2018. Towards empathetic open-domain conversation models: A new benchmark and dataset. *arXiv preprint arXiv:1811.00207*.

Nils Reimers and Iryna Gurevych. 2019. Sentence-bert: Sentence embeddings using siamese bert-networks. In *Proceedings of the 2019 Conference on Empirical Methods in Natural Language Processing*. Association for Computational Linguistics.

Stephen E Robertson, Steve Walker, Susan Jones, Micheline M Hancock-Beaulieu, Mike Gatford, et al. 1995. Okapi at trec-3. *Nist Special Publication Sp*, 109:109.

Gerard Salton and Christopher Buckley. 1988. Term-weighting approaches in automatic text retrieval. *Information processing & management*, 24(5):513–523.

Jaehyung Seo, Seounghoon Lee, Chanjun Park, Yoonna Jang, Hyeonseok Moon, Sugyeong Eo, Seonmin Koo, and Heui-Seok Lim. 2022. A dog is passing over the jet? a text-generation dataset for korean commonsense reasoning and evaluation. In *Findings of the Association for Computational Linguistics: NAACL 2022*, pages 2233–2249.

Haoyu Song, Yan Wang, Kaiyan Zhang, Wei-Nan Zhang, and Ting Liu. 2021. Bob: Bert over bert for training persona-based dialogue models from limited personalized data. *arXiv preprint arXiv:2106.06169*.

Ashish Vaswani, Noam Shazeer, Niki Parmar, Jakob Uszkoreit, Llion Jones, Aidan N Gomez, Łukasz Kaiser, and Illia Polosukhin. 2017. Attention is all you need. *Advances in neural information processing systems*, 30.

Tobias Weyand, Andre Araujo, Bingyi Cao, and Jack Sim. 2020. Google landmarks dataset v2-a large-scale benchmark for instance-level recognition and retrieval. In *Proceedings of the IEEE/CVF conference on computer vision and pattern recognition*, pages 2575–2584.

Houyu Zhang, Zhenghao Liu, Chenyan Xiong, and Zhiyuan Liu. 2019. Grounded conversation generation as guided traverses in commonsense knowledge graphs. *arXiv preprint arXiv:1911.02707*.

Saizheng Zhang, Emily Dinan, Jack Urbanek, Arthur Szlam, Douwe Kiela, and Jason Weston. 2018. Personalizing dialogue agents: I have a dog, do you have pets too? *arXiv preprint arXiv:1801.07243*.

Xueliang Zhao, Wei Wu, Can Xu, Chongyang Tao, Dongyan Zhao, and Rui Yan. 2020. Knowledge-grounded dialogue generation with pre-trained language models. *arXiv preprint arXiv:2010.08824*.

Chujie Zheng, Yunbo Cao, Daxin Jiang, and Minlie Huang. 2020. Difference-aware knowledge selection for knowledge-grounded conversation generation. *arXiv preprint arXiv:2009.09378*.

Hao Zhou, Tom Young, Minlie Huang, Haizhou Zhao, Jingfang Xu, and Xiaoyan Zhu. 2018a. Commonsense knowledge aware conversation generation with graph attention. In *IJCAI*, pages 4623–4629.

Kangyan Zhou, Shrimai Prabhumoye, and Alan W Black. 2018b. A dataset for document grounded conversations. *arXiv preprint arXiv:1809.07358*.

A Statistics of FoCus

	Train	Validation
# Dialogues	11,562	1,445
# Average Rounds	6.00	6.00
Average. Len. Human's Utterance	40.94	40.89
Average. Len. Machine's Utterance	141.13	145.42
# Knowedge-Only Answer	35,580	4,501
# Persona-Knowledge Answer	33,792	4,169
# Landmarks	5,082	1,305

Table 5: Statistics of FoCus (Jang et al., 2022).

B Overview of baseline model architecture.

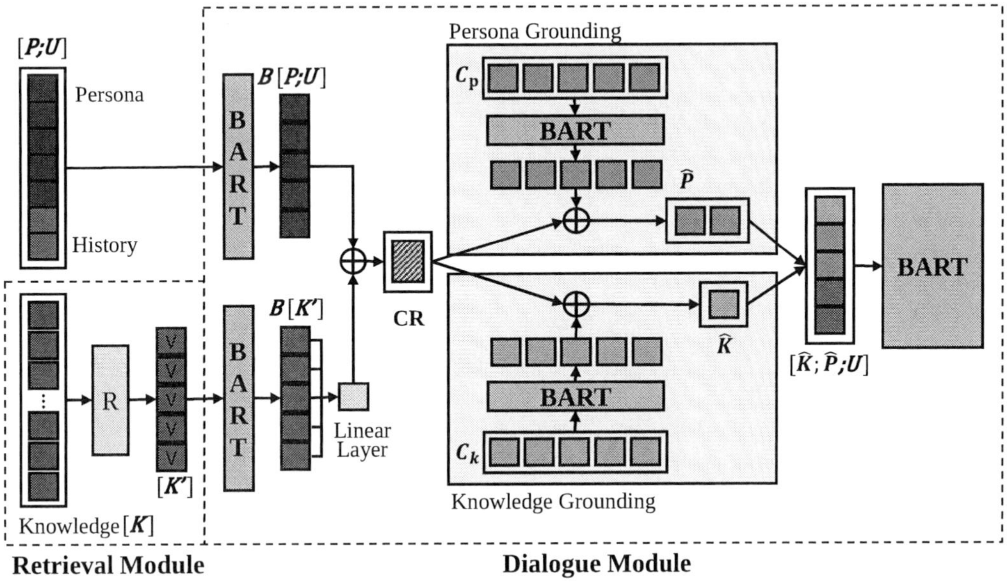

Figure 1: Architecture of proposed FoCus model using BART.

C Details of Knowledge Selection

This is an example of which knowledge is selected when the retrieval module is replaced with each of the TF-IDF, BM25, DPR, and STS modules. STS uses the `multi-qa-MiniLM-L6-dot-v1`[2] pre-trained model provided by Sentence-Transformer (Reimers and Gurevych, 2019) and uses the dot product for embedding of knowledge and user's utterance as a score.

User's Utterance: Where is this place?	
Knowledge	Model Selection
There were ten themed areas by the early 1980s. WaterWorld, ...	TF-IDF, STS
Six Flags purchased AstroWorld in 1975. The next year, Six Flags . . .	TF-IDF
WaterWorld opened in June 1983. The 10-acre 1.9 million-gallon water park . . .	TF-IDF
Peak attendance reached approximately 20,000 people on Saturdays. . . .	TF-IDF
The park had other seasonal attractions such as Alice Cooper's Brutal ...	TF-IDF
Roy Hofheinz acquired and developed 116 acres (47 ha) of land, . . .	BM25, DPR
While the original amusement park site was 57 acres, the Houston ...	BM25, STS
Six Flags AstroWorld, also known simply as AstroWorld, was a seasonally ..	BM25
AstroWorld was permanently closed by Six Flags after its final day of . . .	BM25
Thunder River was installed in 1980, has been described as the "first ...	BM25
An 8-foot (2.4) by 10-foot (3.0) 1967 model of Astroworld ...	DPR, STS
AstroWorld opened to the public with 50,000 guests visiting the first . . .	DPR
XLR-8 was installed in 1984. Looping Starship was installed in 1986. Ultra ...	DPR
Serial Thriller originally operated at AstroWorld starting in 1999. The ride . . .	DPR
In 2009, the former Astroworld site was still vacant. The land tract ...	STS
As of 2018, the HLSR owned the property at the former AstroWorld ...	STS
"Astrodomain" refers to an area of south Houston surrounding . . .	-
Hofheinz developed Astroworld just to the south of the Astrodome. . . .	-
During Astroworld's first twenty years, it entertained more than . . .	-
On September 12, 2005, Six Flags CEO Kieran Burke announced . . .	-
The final date of park operation was October 30, 2005. Following . . .	-
Other features included:	-
The Alpine Sleigh Ride, Astrowheel, and Mill Pond were among ...	-
Bamboo Shoot (formerly Ozarka Splash) was installed in 1969. Installed ...	-
The park's Southern Star Amphitheater opened in 1980 and hosted a . . .	-
Six Flags AstroWorld originated the "Fright Nights" special event . . .	-
Dan Dunn and Jeff Martin worked as a caricaturists at the park. Daniel ...	-
In 2018, former employees organized the AstroWorld 50th Anniversary ...	-

Table 6: Examples of Knowledge Selection in TF-IDF, BM25, DPR, and STS retrieval modules. The table is the result of the selected top-5 knowledge.

[2]https://huggingface.co/sentence-transformers/multi-qa-MiniLM-L6-dot-v1

Proto-Gen: An end-to-end neural generator for persona and knowledge grounded response generation

Sougata Saha, Souvik Das, Rohini Srihari
State University of New York at Buffalo
Department of Computer Science and Engineering
{sougatas, souvikda, rohini}@buffalo.edu

Abstract

In this paper we detail the implementation of Proto-Gen, an end-to-end neural response generator capable of selecting appropriate persona and fact sentences from available options, and generating persona and fact grounded responses. Incorporating a novel interaction layer in an encoder-decoder architecture, Proto-Gen facilitates learning dependencies between facts, persona and the context, and outperforms existing baselines on the FoCus dataset for both the sub-tasks of persona and fact selection, and response generation. We further fine tune Proto-Gen's hyperparameters, and share our results and findings.

1 Introduction

With the growth of neural methods for language modelling, the task of response generation in the field of open domain dialogue and interactive systems have witnessed significant improvements. Incorporating transformer (Vaswani et al., 2017) based architectures with billions of parameters, and trained on large training corpora, such models (Radford et al., 2019; Zhang et al., 2020; Roller et al., 2021; Xu et al., 2022) have advanced the state-of-the-art in response generation. However, trained with the objective of generating the next response by conditioning only on the context, such models often result in unnatural and hallucinated responses (Rashkin et al., 2021), which if not addressed appropriately, hampers it's usefulness in practical settings (Saha et al., 2021).

Although recent years have witnessed advancements in response generators which can factor in external knowledge (Dinan et al., 2019; Gopalakrishnan et al., 2019) and exhibit certain human-like features like personality traits, emotions, .etc (Mairesse and Walker, 2007; Zhang et al., 2018; Rashkin et al., 2019; Saha et al., 2022), research in response generators that can generate user-centric responses by factoring both user persona and external knowledge is still an unsolved problem. In this paper we propose Proto-Gen, an end-to-end response generator that can select the most appropriate fact and user persona sentences based on the conversation context, and generate a response customized for the user.

2 Task an Data Description

The task aims at engendering intelligent response generators that can generate appropriate response to user queries by factoring in the user's persona along with available external facts. It is further divided into two sub-tasks:

- Persona sentences and knowledge prediction: With the inputs being 5 persona candidates of the user, 10 knowledge candidates pertaining to the topic of discussion, and the conversation context, this sub-task requires predicting the correct persona and knowledge sentence which can be used for generating the response.
- Response generation: This sub-task requires generating the agent response to the user query in natural language, using persona and knowledge sentences.

The dataset (Jang et al., 2022) comprises 14,452 persona-knowledge dialogues (11,562 training, 1,445 validation, and 1,445 testing) pertaining to discussions about landmarks such as Statue of Liberty, Eiffel Tower, The Great Wall, etc.

3 Methods

As illustrated in Figure 1, we implement an end-to-end encoder-decoder based architecture for jointly performing all sub-tasks. Below we discuss each component in detail.

3.1 Encoding

The encoding layer comprises two BART (Lewis et al., 2020) based encoders: (i) **Query Encoder**

Proceedings of the 29th International Conference on Computational Linguistic, pages 9–14
October 12–17, 2022.

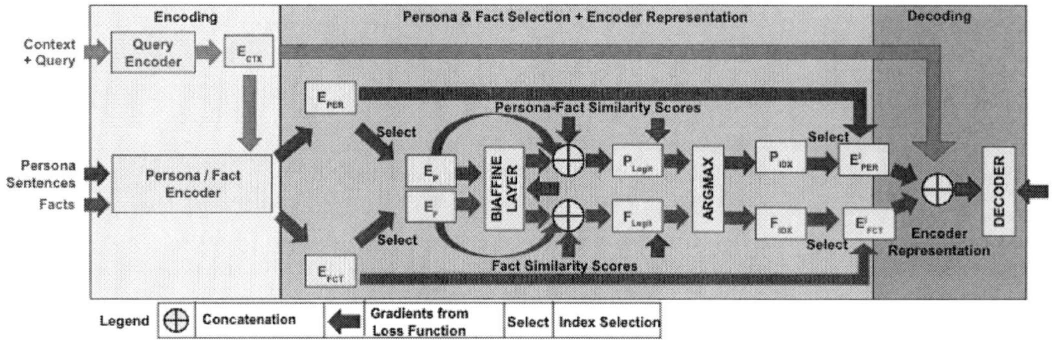

Figure 1: Proto-Gen End-to-End Model Architecture.

for encoding the conversation context and query. (ii) **Persona/Fact Encoder** for sequentially encoding the available persona and fact sentences. First the query encoder $\mathrm{Q\_Enc}$ encodes the context CTX, which comprises the last 128 tokens of the concatenated previous turns and the current user query (Equation 1). The persona and fact encoder $\mathrm{PF\_Enc}$ sequentially encodes each of the 5 persona and 10 knowledge sentences, which are further combined with the encoded context $\mathrm{E_{CTX}}$ using multi-headed attention MHA followed by dropout Drop (Equations 2 to 5), to yield the final persona and fact encodings $\mathrm{E_{PER}}$ and $\mathrm{E_{FCT}}$.

$$\mathrm{E_{CTX}} = \mathrm{Q\_Enc(CTX)} \tag{1}$$

$$\mathrm{E_{PER}} = \mathrm{PF\_Enc(P^i)}|_{\mathrm{i=1}}^{5} \tag{2}$$

$$\mathrm{E_{FCT}} = \mathrm{PF\_Enc(F^i)}|_{\mathrm{i=1}}^{10} \tag{3}$$

$$\mathrm{E_{PER}} = \mathrm{E^i_{PER}} + \mathrm{Drop(MHA(E^i_{PER}, E_{CTX}))}|_{\mathrm{i=1}}^{5} \tag{4}$$

$$\mathrm{E_{FCT}} = \mathrm{E^i_{FCT}} + \mathrm{Drop(MHA(E^i_{FCT}, E_{CTX}))}|_{\mathrm{i=1}}^{10} \tag{5}$$

3.2 Interaction Layer

The interaction layer captures interactions between the context and the presented persona and fact sentences, for determining the best suited persona and fact sentences for generating the current response. The layer inputs the encoded context $\mathrm{E_{CTX}}$, persona $\mathrm{E_{PER}}$ and fact sentences $\mathrm{E_{FCT}}$, and outputs a final concatenated representation $\mathrm{E_{ENC}}$ for the decoder.

For determining the most appropriate persona and fact sentences for the current turn's response, the interaction layer utilizes fully-connected neural networks (FNN) which input a concatenated representation of:

1. Biaffine Interaction Logits: The logits sc from a biaffine classifier which captures the interactions between the input persona and fact sentences. Biaffine classifiers are generalizations of linear classifiers, which include multiplicative interactions between two vectors (Dozat and Manning, 2016). Hence, we incorporate a biaffine layer for jointly determining the most appropriate persona and fact sentences for the current turn. Using layers of FNNs, the embedding of the start-of-sequence (SOS) token of both the fact and persona sentences are transformed to a reduced hidden size, which in turn are passed through a biaffine classifier to predict the most appropriate pair of persona and fact sentences for response generation (Equations 6 to 9). This layer is trained by minimizing the binary cross-entropy (BCE) loss between the predicted logits and the actual labels (Equation 16).

2. Persona & Fact Prior Logits: Depicted in Equations 10 and 11, FNNs are used to compute the prior probability of independently selecting each persona and fact sentence in the current turn. The FNNs inputs the representative persona and fact vectors $\mathrm{E_P}$ and $\mathrm{E_F}$ and yields the logits $\mathrm{FNN(E_P)}$ and $\mathrm{FNN(E_F)}$ for each sentence.

3. Pre-computed Similarity Vector: We input two additional vectors comprising normalized Levenshtein based similarity scores [1], which act as biases. (i) $\mathrm{F_{sim}}$: A vector comprising unit normalized similarity scores between each factual sentence and the available Wikipedia knowledge for the landmark of discussion. (ii) $\mathrm{P_{sim}}$: A vector comprising unit normalized similarity scores between the most similar fact from step (i), and the available persona sentences.

Equations 10 and 11 details the fact and persona prediction sub-tasks, which are trained by minimiz-

[1] https://pypi.org/project/fuzzywuzzy/

ing the BCE loss functions (Equations 18 and 19). Finally, the interaction layer engenders the final representation of the encoding step by concatenating the encoded context E_{CTX}, and the encodings of the most likely persona and fact sentences (Equations 12 to 14).

$$\text{Get}(X, \text{idx}) = X[\text{idx}, :] \tag{6}$$

$$E_P = \text{Get}(E_{PER}, 0);\ E_F = \text{Get}(E_{FCT}, 0) \tag{7}$$

$$\text{Biaf}(x, y) = x^T U y + W(x \oplus y) + b \tag{8}$$

$$\text{sc} = \text{Biaf}(\text{FNN}(E_P), \text{FNN}(E_F)) \tag{9}$$

$$P_{\text{logit}} = \text{FNN}(\text{Cat}(\text{FNN}(E_P), \text{sc}, P_{\text{sim}})) \tag{10}$$

$$F_{\text{logit}} = \text{FNN}(\text{Cat}(\text{FNN}(E_F), \text{sc}, F_{\text{sim}})) \tag{11}$$

$$E_{PER}^{\text{idx}} = \text{Get}(E_{PER}, \text{argmax}(P_{\text{logit}})) \tag{12}$$

$$E_{FCT}^{\text{idx}} = \text{Get}(E_{FCT}, \text{argmax}(F_{\text{logit}})) \tag{13}$$

$$E_{ENC} = \text{Cat}(E_{CTX}, E_{PER}^{\text{idx}}, E_{FCT}^{\text{idx}}) \tag{14}$$

3.3 Decoding and Loss Function

We reuse BART's decoder layers for decoding, where the concatenated representation E_{ENC} is input to the decoder for generating the final response y_{pred} (Equation 15). Depicted in Equation 20, we train the model end-to-end by minimizing the aggregated interpolated loss across all sub-tasks with interpolation factors α, β and γ_1/γ_2 for language modelling loss (Equation 17), persona-fact biaffine interaction prediction loss, and persona/fact selection loss respectively. In order to enhance response generation, we also add an extra penalty term δ with interpolation factor λ to the aggregated loss function, which is set to be proportional to the ratio of salient tokens that are missing from the generated response, with the salient tokens being the nouns, adjectives and verbs in the golden response, which are pre-computed using Spacy [2].

$$y_{\text{pred}} = \text{Decoder}(E_{ENC}) \tag{15}$$

$$\mathcal{L}^{\text{biaf}} = \text{BCE}(y_{\text{biaf}}, \text{sc}) \tag{16}$$

$$\mathcal{L}^{\text{LM}} = \text{CE}(y_{\text{act}}, y_{\text{pred}}) \tag{17}$$

$$\mathcal{L}^{\text{PER}} = \text{BCE}(P_{\text{act}}, P_{\text{logit}}) \tag{18}$$

$$\mathcal{L}^{\text{FCT}} = \text{BCE}(F_{\text{act}}, F_{\text{logit}}) \tag{19}$$

$$\mathcal{L} = \alpha\mathcal{L}^{\text{LM}} + \beta\mathcal{L}^{\text{biaf}} + \gamma_1\mathcal{L}^{\text{PER}} + \gamma_2\mathcal{L}^{\text{FCT}} + \lambda\delta \tag{20}$$

[2]https://spacy.io/usage/linguistic-features

4 Experiments and Results

4.1 Experiment Setup

We use BART (Lewis et al., 2020) as the base encoder, and increase its embedding layer to accommodate two special tokens <agent_1>, <agent_2> to distinguish between speaker turns, and two tokens <persona>, <knowledge> to distinguish between persona and factual sentences. Four layers comprising four attention heads are used for multi-headed attention in the interaction layer. The hidden size of the FNNs in the biaffine layer is set to 600. All models are trained with a learning rate of 1e-5 for 15 epochs and optimised using AdamW (Loshchilov and Hutter, 2017), with early stopping if the validation loss doesn't reduce for 2 epochs. Further, a weight of 5.0 is applied to positive examples during computing binary cross entropy loss for the biaffine prediction. The interpolation factors $\alpha, \beta, \gamma_1, \gamma_2$ and λ are set to 0.6, 0.1, 0.1, 0.1, and 0.1 respectively by default.

4.2 Experiments

We experiment with different hyperparameter settings to engender multiple variants of the model. Specifically, we experiment with (i) Adding/removing the additional persona and fact similarity score vector as inputs in the interaction layer, (ii) Adding/removing the keyword based penalty term δ in the final model loss (Equation 20), (iii) Using both the base and large versions of pre-trained BART, (iv) Adding dropout with a probability of 0.1 for regularization post concatenating the biaffine interaction logits, persona & fact prior logits and the pre-computed similarity vector in the interaction layer, (v) Sharing the same base encoder for encoding fact and persona sentences, (vi) Different values of the interpolation factor. Table 1 lists all the different hyperparameter settings that we experiment with, along with the resultant model ids.

4.3 Results and Observations

We train and evaluate all the model variants on the standard training and evaluation splits of the FoCus (Jang et al., 2022) dataset. For persona and knowledge selection (sub-task 1), we report overall accuracy scores-Persona Accuracy and Knowledge Accuracy, as well as Average Grounding-an average of the two accuracy scores. For response generation (sub-task 2), we report SacreBLEU (Post, 2018), CharF++ (Popović, 2015) and ROUGE-L

Model ID	Similarity Scores	Keyword Penalty	Base Model	Add Dropout	Persona & Fact Shared Encoder	Interpolation Factors
1	yes	no	bart-base	yes	yes	0.7, 0.05, 0.15, 0.1, 0.0
2	yes	no	bart-base	yes	yes	0.6, 0.2, 0.1, 0.1, 0.0
3	yes	no	bart-base	yes	no	0.6, 0.2, 0.1, 0.1, 0.0
4	yes	no	bart-base	no	yes	0.6, 0.2, 0.1, 0.1, 0.0
5	yes	no	bart-large	no	yes	0.6, 0.2, 0.1, 0.1, 0.0
6	yes	yes	bart-base	no	yes	0.6, 0.1, 0.1, 0.1, 0.1
7	no	yes	bart-base	no	yes	0.6, 0.1, 0.1, 0.1, 0.1

Table 1: List of experiments with different hyperparameter settings

Model ID	Persona Accuracy	Knowledge Accuracy	Average Grounding	Sacre BLEU	Char F++	ROUGE L	Average Generation	Average Score
(Jang et al., 2022)*	86.86	65.06	75.96	10.87	27.90	30.99	23.26	49.61
1	77.26	32.49	54.87	8.58	28.08	21.81	19.49	37.18
2	86.38	80.36	83.37	18.91	40.07	38.03	32.34	57.85
3	86.16	74.24	80.20	18.19	40.10	36.27	31.52	55.86
4	85.02	**85.18**	**85.10**	**19.85**	**42.32**	**38.84**	**33.67**	**59.39**
5	**87.75**	68.72	78.23	18.35	39.68	38.14	32.06	55.14
6	84.00	83.09	83.54	19.28	41.74	38.14	33.05	58.30
7	85.35	79.42	82.39	19.39	41.90	38.00	33.10	57.74

Table 2: Results of the experiments from Table 1. The best score for each metric is highlighted in bold. * lists the best scores from the external baseline.

(Lin, 2004) scores, along with an aggregated metric of all the three metrics-Average Generation. We also report Average Score-an overall metric for both the sub-tasks by averaging the Average Grounding and Average Generation scores.

Table 2 shares the results of the experiments listed in Table 1. We make the following observations: (i) Comparing models 4 and 5, we observe that using bart-base as the base model generally outperforms bart-large, which we attribute to the smaller size of training data in comparison to the larger number of parameter updates requires to train the large model. (ii) Comparing models 6 and 7, we see that incorporating the persona and fact similarity scores as additional vectors mostly results in better scores. This intuitively makes sense, as the similarity vector acts as an additional bias term for the model, which facilitates learning. (iii) Comparing models 4 and 6, we observe that adding the keyword based penalty term to the loss function does not seem to help learning. (iv) In comparison to model 4, adding dropout to the concatenated representation of the interaction layer in model 2 does not yield better results. We reason that since the base architecture already includes multiple regularization constrains, adding additional dropout layers hinders learning, specially because the size of the training data is small compared to the pre-training data of BART. (v) Comparing models 2 and 3, we observe that sharing the base encoder for encoding both persona and fact sentences, results in better scores. We attribute this to the fewer parameter updates required for parameter sharing. (vi) Comparing models 1 and 2, we note that a higher interpolation factor for biaffine classifier yields better overall scores, in comparison to fact and persona selection. Overall, we observe that model 4, which uses bart-base as the base model, inputs the additional similarity vectors, shares encoder for encoding persona and fact, while not adding additional dropout and keyword penalty, yields best results on the validation set.

5 Conclusion

Here we detail Proto-Gen, an end-to-end neural response generator, that can not only select appropriate persona and fact sentences from available input options, but also generate persona and knowledge grounded responses. Incorporating a novel interaction layer which includes biaffine classifiers and trained on the FoCus dataset, Proto-Gen outperforms existing external baselines for all sub-tasks. We further perform experiments to fine tune Proto-Gen's hyperparameters, and report our results.

References

Emily Dinan, Stephen Roller, Kurt Shuster, Angela Fan, Michael Auli, and Jason Weston. 2019. Wizard of Wikipedia: Knowledge-powered conversational agents. In *Proceedings of the International Conference on Learning Representations (ICLR)*.

Timothy Dozat and Christopher D. Manning. 2016. Deep biaffine attention for neural dependency parsing.

Karthik Gopalakrishnan, Behnam Hedayatnia, Qinlang Chen, Anna Gottardi, Sanjeev Kwatra, Anu Venkatesh, Raefer Gabriel, and Dilek Hakkani-Tür. 2019. Topical-Chat: Towards Knowledge-Grounded Open-Domain Conversations. In *Proc. Interspeech 2019*, pages 1891–1895.

Yoonna Jang, Jungwoo Lim, Yuna Hur, Dongsuk Oh, Suhyune Son, Yeonsoo Lee, Donghoon Shin, Seungryong Kim, and Heuiseok Lim. 2022. Call for customized conversation: Customized conversation grounding persona and knowledge. *Proceedings of the AAAI Conference on Artificial Intelligence*, 36(10):10803–10812.

Mike Lewis, Yinhan Liu, Naman Goyal, Marjan Ghazvininejad, Abdelrahman Mohamed, Omer Levy, Veselin Stoyanov, and Luke Zettlemoyer. 2020. BART: Denoising sequence-to-sequence pre-training for natural language generation, translation, and comprehension. In *Proceedings of the 58th Annual Meeting of the Association for Computational Linguistics*, pages 7871–7880, Online. Association for Computational Linguistics.

Chin-Yew Lin. 2004. ROUGE: A package for automatic evaluation of summaries. In *Text Summarization Branches Out*, pages 74–81, Barcelona, Spain. Association for Computational Linguistics.

Ilya Loshchilov and Frank Hutter. 2017. Decoupled weight decay regularization.

François Mairesse and Marilyn Walker. 2007. PERSONAGE: Personality generation for dialogue. In *Proceedings of the 45th Annual Meeting of the Association of Computational Linguistics*, pages 496–503, Prague, Czech Republic. Association for Computational Linguistics.

Maja Popović. 2015. chrF: character n-gram F-score for automatic MT evaluation. In *Proceedings of the Tenth Workshop on Statistical Machine Translation*, pages 392–395, Lisbon, Portugal. Association for Computational Linguistics.

Matt Post. 2018. A call for clarity in reporting BLEU scores. In *Proceedings of the Third Conference on Machine Translation: Research Papers*, pages 186–191, Belgium, Brussels. Association for Computational Linguistics.

Alec Radford, Jeffrey Wu, Rewon Child, David Luan, Dario Amodei, Ilya Sutskever, et al. 2019. Language models are unsupervised multitask learners. *OpenAI blog*, 1(8):9.

Hannah Rashkin, David Reitter, Gaurav Singh Tomar, and Dipanjan Das. 2021. Increasing faithfulness in knowledge-grounded dialogue with controllable features. In *Proceedings of the 59th Annual Meeting of the Association for Computational Linguistics and the 11th International Joint Conference on Natural Language Processing (Volume 1: Long Papers)*, pages 704–718, Online. Association for Computational Linguistics.

Hannah Rashkin, Eric Michael Smith, Margaret Li, and Y-Lan Boureau. 2019. Towards empathetic open-domain conversation models: A new benchmark and dataset. In *Proceedings of the 57th Annual Meeting of the Association for Computational Linguistics*, pages 5370–5381, Florence, Italy. Association for Computational Linguistics.

Stephen Roller, Emily Dinan, Naman Goyal, Da Ju, Mary Williamson, Yinhan Liu, Jing Xu, Myle Ott, Eric Michael Smith, Y-Lan Boureau, and Jason Weston. 2021. Recipes for building an open-domain chatbot. *Proceedings of the 16th Conference of the European Chapter of the Association for Computational Linguistics: Main Volume.*

Sougata Saha, Souvik Das, Elizabeth Soper, Erin Pacquetet, and Rohini K. Srihari. 2021. Proto: A neural cocktail for generating appealing conversations.

Sougata Saha, Souvik Das, and Rohini Srihari. 2022. Stylistic response generation by controlling personality traits and intent. In *Proceedings of the 4th Workshop on NLP for Conversational AI*, pages 197–211, Dublin, Ireland. Association for Computational Linguistics.

Ashish Vaswani, Noam Shazeer, Niki Parmar, Jakob Uszkoreit, Llion Jones, Aidan N Gomez, Ł ukasz Kaiser, and Illia Polosukhin. 2017. Attention is all you need. In *Advances in Neural Information Processing Systems*, volume 30. Curran Associates, Inc.

Jing Xu, Arthur Szlam, and Jason Weston. 2022. Beyond goldfish memory: Long-term open-domain conversation. *Proceedings of the 60th Annual Meeting of the Association for Computational Linguistics (Volume 1: Long Papers).*

Saizheng Zhang, Emily Dinan, Jack Urbanek, Arthur Szlam, Douwe Kiela, and Jason Weston. 2018. Personalizing dialogue agents: I have a dog, do you have pets too? In *Proceedings of the 56th Annual Meeting of the Association for Computational Linguistics (Volume 1: Long Papers)*, pages 2204–2213, Melbourne, Australia. Association for Computational Linguistics.

Yizhe Zhang, Siqi Sun, Michel Galley, Yen-Chun Chen, Chris Brockett, Xiang Gao, Jianfeng Gao, Jingjing Liu, and Bill Dolan. 2020. DIALOGPT : Large-scale generative pre-training for conversational response generation. In *Proceedings of the 58th Annual Meeting of the Association for Computational Linguistics: System Demonstrations*, pages 270–278, Online. Association for Computational Linguistics.

Evaluating Agent Interactions Through Episodic Knowledge Graphs

Selene Báez Santamaría and **Piek Vossen** and **Thomas Baier**
Vrije University Amsterdam
{s.baezsantamaria, p.t.j.m.vossen, t.baier}@vu.nl

Abstract

We present a new method based on episodic Knowledge Graphs (eKGs) for evaluating (multimodal) conversational agents in open domains. This graph is generated by interpreting raw signals during conversation and is able to capture the accumulation of knowledge over time. We apply structural and semantic analysis of the resulting graphs and translate the properties into qualitative measures. We compare these measures with existing automatic and manual evaluation metrics commonly used for conversational agents. Our results show that our Knowledge-Graph-based evaluation provides more qualitative insights into interaction and the agent's behavior.

1 Introduction

In order to develop open-domain conversational agents, it is crucial to have automatic and reproducible ways of evaluating the interaction and the agent's role. However, interaction with people is challenging to evaluate for several reasons: 1) people behave differently in each interaction, 2) people appreciate the interaction for different reasons and aspects, 3) different goals and sub-goals may play a role simultaneously, and 4) personal relationships and past experiences have an impact on every interaction. For these reasons, most evaluations of interactive systems use human judges and questionnaires in analogy to user-satisfaction methods.

In addition to these questionnaires, conversational systems are often evaluated by comparing system responses to human responses on a turn-by-turn basis, where the prompts and the gold responses are taken from human-human conversations. Standard measures such as BLUE (Papineni et al., 2002), METEOR (Banerjee and Lavie, 2005), BERTscore (Zhang* et al., 2020) test the similarity between the system response and a gold response, whereas USR (Mehri and Eskenazi, 2020) tests the coherence of the system response to the previous prompt and context. However, these measures do not truly assess the quality of the system's interpretation and the relevance of the prompt, and they *punish systems for being creative and making responses personal.* By detaching prompt-response pairs from the whole conversation, these metrics evaluate the reactivity of an agent, not its ability to engage in a coherent interaction.

Deriu et al. (2021) mention five general requirements for evaluation: 1) automatic to reduce human labour and subjectivity, 2) repeatable when applied to the same dialogue, 3) correlate with human judgments, 4) differentiated for various strategies, and 5) explainable. None of the existing approaches satisfy all these criteria. In this paper, we demonstrate that graph properties can be used as an additional and independent evaluation of the **effectiveness** of the communication. This evaluation is an automatic measure of **semantic quality** that is also explainable and reproducible, meeting three of the five previous requirements.

We present a novel evaluation method that qualifies conversations using an episodic Knowledge Graph (eKG) (Baez Santamaria et al., 2021). We calibrate different groups of graph measures in relation to human evaluations and ground truth independent measures. To test our selected metrics, we compare the quality of types of conversations and show that the proposed evaluation framework holds, regardless of differences in system design. Our contributions are:

1. We provide an reference-free and explainable method for evaluating the interaction of conversational agents.
2. We compare our method to other standard evaluation methods and show its complementary value.
3. We demonstrate that our method can be applied across multiple conversations and different (types of) participants.

Proceedings of the 29th International Conference on Computational Linguistic, pages 15–28
October 12–17, 2022.

2 Related work

Dialogue systems have been studied for several decades and are further developed within Conversational AI systems. In their survey, Deriu et al. (2021) discuss different types of dialogue systems and how they are evaluated. They conclude that evaluating open conversational agents is an open problem due to the lack of a goal and variable structure. Therefore, evaluation approaches focus on appropriateness and human likeness of responses or specific linguistic properties such as variability, lexical complexity, coherence, correctness, and relevance of system responses. Evaluations can furthermore be done at a turn-level or conversation-level. There is a many-to-many problem in both cases: multiple responses can be correct, multiple dialogues can lead to the right/same result, and every interaction is unique.

Attempts to automate these notions often rely on metrics such as BLUE (Papineni et al., 2002), ROUGE (Lin and Och, 2004), METEOR (Banerjee and Lavie, 2005), and BERTscore (Zhang* et al., 2020) to measure the similarity of the agent response to one or more ground-truth responses; or they borrow from information retrieval measures when systems need to select the appropriate responses from a set of possible alternatives. In contrast, USR (Mehri and Eskenazi, 2020) is a new method created by fine-tuning RoBERTa-base (Liu et al., 2019) on the training set of Topical-Chat. Whereas METEOR and BERTscore compare a system response to a ground-truth response, USR gives a quality evaluation score without a ground-truth response (reference-free) by measuring the coherence of the system response with the human prompt and the previous context.

Evaluation regimes with ground-truth responses limit agents' "freedom and creativity" to generate other responses that may also fit the purpose. Therefore, it is unsurprising that evaluations often fall back on a posteriori evaluation by human judges. However, human evaluations suffer from several pitfalls: expensive, time-consuming, inconsistent across experiments, difficult to reproduce, and challenging to scale. Researchers tried to harmonize the evaluation criteria to address the inconsistency and lack of coherence in terminology and methodology for human evaluations of open-domain dialogue. Howcroft et al. (2020) survey of 165 papers with human evaluations reports more than 200 quality criteria (such as Fluency, Accuracy, or Readability.) that have been used in Natural Language Generation. Independently, Fitrianie et al. (2019) analyzed the proceedings of the conference of Intelligent Virtual Agents[1] between 2013 and 2018. They found 189 constructs from 89 questionnaires reported in 81 papers, which they reduced to 19 measurement instruments. Measurements range from how enjoyable, correct and useful to how fluent.

In an attempt to automate evaluations and make them more reproducible and scalable, the *Ninth Dialog System Technology Challenge, Track on Interactive Evaluation of Dialog* (DSTC9, Track 3)[2] carried out a variety of automatic and human evaluations on 33 systems submissions to the Topical-Chat challenge (Gopalakrishnan et al., 2019). Topical-Chat consists of conversations between two Amazon Mechanical Turk workers who were given prior knowledge or information to refer to during their conversation. Systems need to respond to turns from these conversations, replacing one worker. A human evaluation of system responses was done using the questionnaire from the FED dataset (Mehri and Eskenazi). An automatic evaluation was done using the measures METEOR, BERTscore, and USR. Gunasekara et al. (2020) report that the USR (0.3 Spearman) correlates better with human judgments than METEOR (0.23 Spearman) and BERTscore (Spearman 0.22), although they also admit that the correlation is not very high. It is still to be seen how easy USR can be transferred to other dialogues and contexts, as it was trained and tested on Topical-Chat.

We present a reference-free approach that is not based on coherence but measures the interpretability of (multimodal) situations and accumulates these over time. The basic idea is that effective interactions result in rich and high-quality representations that can be measured in a Knowledge Graph. Factors determining the communication effect are the agent's response quality and the collaboration between participants.

3 Problem formalization

We represent an interaction as a series of tuples *[t, s, g, f, p]*, such that:

t $\in$ **T**, a set of time points

s $\in$ **S**, a set of situations

g $\in$ **G**, a set of graphs

[1]https://dl.acm.org/conference/iva/proceedings

[2]http://dialog.speech.cs.cmu.edu:8003

$\mathbf{f} \in \mathbf{F}$, a set of unknown features part of situation **s**

$\mathbf{p} \in \mathbf{P}$, a set of defined properties that can make up graph **g**

A graph **g** represents the interpretation of a sequence of situations **s** at time point **t**. Each situation **s** can be modeled as a bundle of unknown features **f** and each graph **g** as a set of properties **p** that are defined a priori. To quality the conversations, we measure how many and which properties **p** are extracted from each turn and the cumulative effect of adding these properties over time to the graph **g**. The instrument's effectiveness in measuring quality depends on the ability to detect the properties **p** given the features **f**. The effectiveness of the communication depends on the predefined properties **p** that are chosen for the evaluation.

The properties used to define the quality of the conversation can be 1) mathematical, e.g. measuring the average degree and sparseness, 2) semantic, e.g. number and type of triples, 3) knowledge integrity, e.g. conflicts, outliers, analogies, completeness, 4) subjective values, e.g. sentiment and emotion, certainty, trust, and 5) dialogue properties, e.g. turn-property ratio's, utterance type distribution and density, style and quality of expression. These measures depend on the capability to extract **p** from the unknown features **f** -implicit in image, audio and text signals- and the modelling of these properties in the knowledge graph **g**. An interaction will result in a series of graphs over time. A cumulative graph can be seen as an episodic Knowledge Graph (eKG) (Baez Santamaria et al., 2021) for which the qualitative evaluation over time can provide valuable additional insight.

In this paper, we implement the above formal model and propose a set of properties **p**, defined as RDF triples, that correlate with human judgements and can be used across different conversational setups and for different property detection systems.

3.1 Model

Figure 1 shows the interpretation of the statement "I like reading 1984" in an eKG. The core triple reflects that "Nicole" "reads" something labelled as "1984". The triple itself is a named graph representing a claim. The claim is mentioned (denotedBy) by the speaker Nicole (attributedTo) and perspective values are attributed to this mention, such as sentiment:positive, polarity:positive, certainty:certain. The model can represent multiple mentions of the same triple, with different perspective values and/or attributed to different speakers.

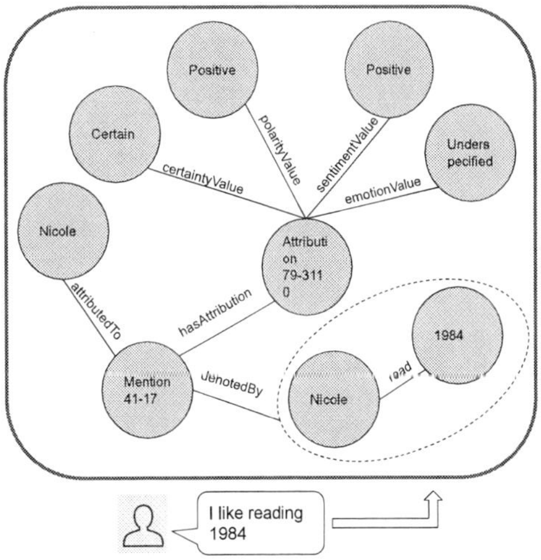

Figure 1: Example of how an utterance is converted into an episodic graph with source perspective values.

4 Capturing interaction and episodic knowledge

In order to apply graph metrics, we need to generate properties from the (multimodal) signals produced during the interaction. As we represent these properties as RDF triples, we rely on a text-to-triple instrument to detect these properties. This instrument's effectiveness determines the evaluation's depth, precision and richness; therefore, the most precise and standardised instrument is preferable. However, using the same instrument across interactions, we can compare the interactions and draw conclusions about its conversational variables.

Another factor for our evaluation is the graph properties modelled in the eKG. Some properties are generic and can be measured in any graph, whereas other properties depend on the semantics of the data model. In the following subsections, we discuss conversational variables when comparing interactions, the metrics that can be applied to the generated graphs and how they depend on specific property types.

4.1 Conversational variables

Our framework is agnostic to an interaction setup. We can thus have various combinations of prompt and response participants, and we can use different triples extractors, as shown in Figure 2. Schematically, the interlocutors (P1 and P2) both produce conversational signals to which we can apply triple-extraction, updating the eKG. Our evaluation framework is applied to this eKG, which

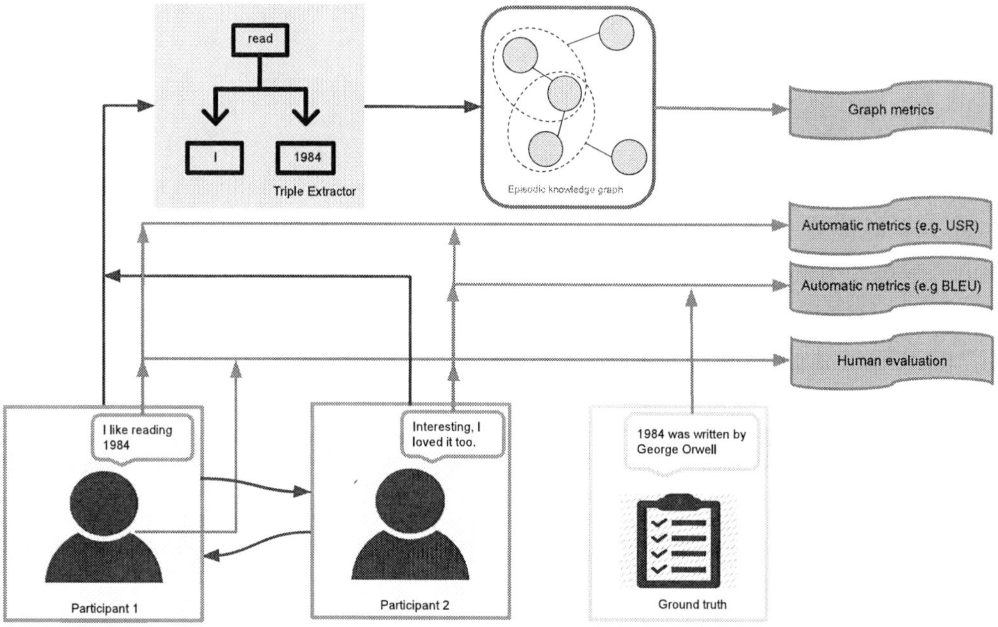

Figure 2: Schematic representation of interaction process (in purple), golden data (in yellow), EKG construction (in blue) and evaluation (in green). Arrows flowing into the metrics determine the components needed for their calculation.

is reference-free and considers the interaction between both interlocutors. This differs from other evaluation frameworks, such as USR, which only evaluates P2 as a coherent response to P1, and BLUE, METEOR and BERTscore, which evaluate P2 against a ground-truth response.

Triple extractor Regardless of the interlocutors, we can apply triple extraction to the utterances a-posteriori and derive an eKG from the communication. The extracted triples represent factoid information and possibly the speakers' perspectives. Some approaches to extract triples are: StandforOpenIE (Angeli et al., 2015), spaCy's Dependency parser (Vasiliev, 2020), or tailored Context Free Grammars (CFG).

Agents As for the type of participants, we can take recorded human-human dialogues and apply triple extraction to each prompt from an actor. Similarly, machine-machine conversations can be generated where a chatbot mimics human input as a *prompt agent* and another chatbot functions as the *response agent*.

4.2 Graph metrics

Our formal model allows us to evaluate conversations under different frameworks: as a mathematical object (group A), as an RDF knowledge representation tool (group B), and as an eKG hosting the accumulation of interactions (group C). For groups A and B we used an implementation by Pernisch et al. (2020) while for groups C we implemented the metrics using *rdflib*.

After an exploratory analysis with 62 graph metrics (A-15, B-27, C-20), we select a subset of 24, as many of these metrics are compositional and therefore correlate highly and mostly reflect the same insights. Our selected Group A metrics include volume (number of nodes and edges), centrality (average node degree, degree centrality, and closeness), connectivity (average degree connectivity and assortativity), clique (number of strong connected components), entropy (centrality and closeness entropy) and density (sparseness). Group B metrics include volume (number of axioms) and density (average population). Finally, Group C metrics include density (ratios comparing claims to triples, perspectives to triples, conflicts to triples, perspectives to claims, mentions to claims, conflicts to claims), and interaction (average perspectives per claim, mentions per claim, turns per interaction, claims per source and perspectives per source).

The above measures can be applied to the evolving eKG during the interaction or a posteriori. Al-

Table 1: Statistics for 9 conversations with the number of turns, claims and perspectives. The conversation effect is measured by the average claim-triples (claim density) and perspective-triples (perspective density) per turn.

Category	P1	P2	Triple Extractor	Turns	Claims	Claim density	Perspective	Perspective density
Human - Machine	Student	Leolani	CFG	83	27	0.33	23	0.28
Human - Machine	Student	Leolani	CFG	57	18	0.32	14	0.25
Human - Machine	Student	Leolani	CFG	45	17	0.38	14	0.31
Human - Machine	Student	Leolani	CFG	55	14	0.25	11	0.20
Human - Machine	Student	Leolani	CFG	78	21	0.27	16	0.21
Human - Machine	Student	Leolani	CFG	80	22	0.28	17	0.21
Machine - Machine	Blenderbot	Leolani	CFG-spacy	298	6	0.02	4	0.01
Machine - Machine	Blenderbot	Eliza	CFG-spacy	207	24	0.12	22	0.11
Human - Human	Monica	Chandler	Stanford-OIE	243	109	0.44	0	0.00

though these measures were not originally intended as quality measures for interaction, we hypothesize that some of these measures can be used to characterize a conversation, and the resulting graphs can be compared independently. For example, the average claims per source may signal how much information the agent is getting per person it interacts with, the ratio of mentions to claims signals how much a factoid has been repeated in conversation, while the ratio of perspectives to claims signals how much diversity of opinions or sentiment has been expressed on claimed factoids.

5 Experimental setup

Table 1 shows an overview of the conversations analyzed. Details on the artificial agents and triple extractors can be found in the Appendix as well as an in-depth analysis of the triples extracted. We calculate the number of claims and the number of perspectives from each session. To measure the overall effectiveness in interpreting the conversation, we derive the density of claims and perspectives per turn[3], which can be seen as the first crude measure of quality.

Human - Machine conversations Three groups of students had two conversations with Leolani (Vossen et al., 2018) during which they had to introduce themselves. Students were instructed to converse for 5 to 10 minutes or 30-40 turns per conversation. They were also instructed about the type of sentences and expressions from which the agent could extract triples to make the conversations more successful. Conversations will be more cumbersome in real open settings where users do not know what the agent can understand.

[3]Note that the number of turns includes Participant 2's responses, while the extraction focuses on claims and perspectives from P1. About half of the total number of turns are utterances from the students, which makes densities of 0.25 and higher still effective.

Machine - Machine conversations We set up dialogues between Blenderbot (Roller et al., 2020) and Leolani, and Blenderbot with Eliza (Weizenbaum, 1966), where we extract triples using a tailored Context Free Grammar (CFG) and spaCy's dependency parses.

Human - Human conversations We take all dyadic dialogues in the Friends dataset (Poria et al., 2018) between Monica and Chandler and extract triples using StanfordOIE (Angeli et al., 2015).

6 Comparing within conversational variables

To measure the quality of multiple interactions across different participants with the same agent, we collected human judgements of the human-machine conversations and compared these with the graph metrics groups.

6.1 Human evaluations

The students evaluated the agent's responses in their conversation using the DSTC9 Track3 challenge evaluation metrics (Mehri et al., 2022), which form three submetric groups: 1) enjoyability (Interesting, Engaging, Specific, Relevant), 2) semantic correctness (Correct, Semantically Appropriate, Understandable), and 3) fluency. Each conversation got between two to four evaluations where students score each turn for all submetrics and overall score. Table 2 shows the aggregated results, showing the averaged scores for all six conversations. Although Leolani has limited communication skills, most ratings fall above mid-range.

Table 3 shows the average overall score (2.73) and the average over the submetrics (2.84), which hints that the submetrics comprehensively indicate the overall appreciation. The submetrics vary across but are close to the overall average. The enjoyable submetrics score lower than the semantic correctness and fluency ones.

Table 2: Human ratings of six conversations. Score range: 1 (very bad) to 5 (very good).

	Conversations					
	1.1	**1.2**	**2.1**	**2.2**	**4.1**	**4.2**
Interesting	2.65	2.97	1.56	1.60	**2.98**	1.91
Engaging	2.79	**3.12**	1.92	2.69	2.94	2.22
Specific	**2.94**	2.84	2.02	2.31	2.68	2.02
Relevant	3.25	**3.86**	2.83	2.76	2.97	2.25
Correct	3.15	**3.93**	2.63	2.55	3.01	2.20
Semantic appr.	3.06	**3.91**	2.44	2.48	2.98	2.27
Understandable	3.75	**4.06**	3.33	3.05	3.31	2.97
Fluent	3.64	**4.13**	2.67	2.45	3.16	3.08
Average submetrics	3.15	**3.60**	2.42	2.49	3.00	2.37
Overall hum.	3.16	**3.41**	2.35	2.57	2.74	2.12

6.2 Automatic evaluations

Following DSTC9-track3, we scored the agent responses using the USR model ("adamlin/usr-topicalchat-roberta_ft"). We implemented a likelihood score (USR LLH) that averages the masked-task prediction of the model for every token in the agent response given the preceding utterances as context (up to 300 characters). For every token, we get the top 20 predictions to get the token's score, or a score of zero if it was not listed. We also average the likelihood of the highest-scoring token (USR MAX) as the perfect response according to the pre-trained model. We normalized the USR scores to a 5-point Likert scale to match it with the human ratings and averaged over all responses and conversations. The response of our agent scores significant lower (USR LLH=1.68) than the Overall Human Rating of the conversations (2.73). The maximal possible score by USR is close the to Overall Human Rating (USR MAX=2.78).

Table 3: Average human ratings. Score range: 1 (very bad) to 5 (very good). Mean Squared Error (MSE) for submetric and USR metric averages against the overall human rating.

		MSE against overall human score		
	Avg	Human	USR LLH	USR MAX
Interesting	2.28	0.05	0.15	0.16
Engaging	2.61	0.06	0.13	0.19
Specific	2.47	0.06	0.13	0.16
Relevant	2.99	0.04	0.13	0.16
Correct	2.91	0.03	0.14	0.13
Semantic appr.	2.86	0.03	0.14	0.15
Understandable	3.41	0.08	0.14	0.15
Fluent	3.19	0.09	0.19	0.18
Average submetrics	2.84	0.05	0.19	0.18
Overall hum.	2.73		0.15	0.16

We measured the Mean Squared Error (MSE) by comparing the USR scores and the human submetrics against the Overall Human Rating. The MSE scores for the human submetrics below 1 point. The USR LLH and USR MAX scores are 2 to 3 times higher but remain below 2 points, which means they deviate less than average from the human norm. Finally, our agent response (USR LLH) in most cases correlates better than the most likely predicted tokens from the model itself (USR MAX).

6.3 Episodic knowledge graph evaluations

The previous evaluations (human questionnaires and automatic USR) do not evaluate the quality of the knowledge communicated. To that end, we apply the graph measures described in Section 4.2 to the eKGs of the student conversations. We compute the correlations between the graph metrics and the human and automatic metrics for each student conversation (Appendix Figure 4). Two patterns are visible: metric group A correlates more strongly with human evaluations, while metric group B correlates with automatic evaluation. Seven of the human metrics correlate the most with the average degree per node in the eKG. The other two human evaluations, Overall Human Rating and Relevance, correlate the most to sparseness.

7 Comparing across conversational variables

Three major factors determine the resulting graph: 1) the (human) participant, 2) the agent's capability to understand the prompts, and 3) the agent's capability to respond adequately. Our eKG-based evaluation, therefore, genuinely evaluates interaction from both ends. This makes it possible to evaluate interaction across different (types of) people with the same and/or different agents, resulting in different graphs due to the human input and/or the agents' capabilities.

7.1 Correlation with human judgements

Table 4 shows the values between human evaluations, automatic evaluations, and the graph metric with highest correlation.[4] For 6/9 human metrics, including Overall Human Rating, two graph metrics correlate more strongly than the USR metrics. We interpret this as evidence for these two graph evaluations to approximate human evaluations instead of USR evaluations. Recall that Gunasekara et al. (2020) reported a correlation of 0.3 for USR concerning the Topical-Chat evaluation, which is higher than the score obtained for our conversations. Since USR was fine-tuned on Topical-Chat

[4]Chatbot conversations have not been evaluated manually.

training data, it is expected to reflect stronger coherence relations on these conversations. Furthermore, Topical-Chat consists of human-human conversations replaced by system responses, whereas our conversations are naturally-born agent conversations that partly come from the inner drives of the agent. The task to generate an appropriate response is more challenging for our agent compared to fine-tuned language models that mimic human responses.

Table 4: Human evaluation, automatic scores and the most correlated graph metric.

	Average degree	Sparseness	USR LLH
Interesting	0.088	0.077	**0.148**
Engaging	**0.158**	0.145	0.076
Specific	**0.124**	0.067	0.072
Relevant	0.055	0.062	**0.091**
Correct	0.071	0.040	**0.128**
Semantically Appropriate	**0.124**	0.076	0.053
Understandable	**0.119**	0.050	-0.013
Fluent	**0.184**	-0.061	-0.039
Overall Human Rating	0.120	**0.194**	0.088

Average degree Average node degree reflects how many edges a node on the eKG has. Figure 3a exposes a relation between average degree and fluency. Conversations 1.2 and 1.1 scored the highest on fluency, while conversation 1.1 shows the lowest average degree curve. In contrast, conversation 2.2 scored the lowest on fluency and showed an incremental behaviour for this metric. Both Blenderbot conversations show a steep increase of the average degree as the conversation proceeds. Manual inspection of these dialogues reveals that Blenderbot becomes repetitive after several turns, resulting in an extreme increase of the average degree. Responses from Leolani are more repetitive than responses from Eliza, which is consistent as Blenderbot is trained with PersonaChat (Zhang et al., 2019), Empathetic Dialogues (Rashkin et al., 2018) and Wikipedia topic conversations (Dinan et al., 2018), making Blenderbot responsive for Eliza's empathic prompts to talk about personal relations and emotions. The responses from Leolani, on the other hand, are based on its drives which can be more obscure and less "human", causing Blenderbot to fall back on standard responses rapidly. Finally, the conversation between Monica and Chandler shows a different pattern, where the degree drops linearly. The fast decreasing curve can be explained by high fluency between (scripted) human-human dialogues.

Sparseness Sparseness reflects how well connected a graph is. Figure 3b shows that, for all conversations, sparseness decreases as the conversation proceeds and the Overall Human Rating get higher as the eKG gets less sparse. Conversation 4.2 has the slowest decaying curve, while conversation 1.1 decays the fastest. Conversation 2.2 plateaus for a few turns, which is reflected by having the lowest Overall Human Rating. Since all eKGs have the same sparseness starting point, this suggests that conversations that fail to expand these initially dense graphs might not be successful. The Blenderbot-Leolani conversation is less steep, suggesting that it is less successful. The Blenderbot-Eliza conversation appears to be very similar in decreasing sparseness to the student-Leolani conversations, thus confirming that Blenderbot and Eliza are well aligned. The most effective conversation is shown by Monica and Chandler, having a curve that decays to the same level as conversation 1.1, but decays further.

7.2 Complementing human judgements

While some metrics correlate with human judgments, other graph metrics complement human evaluations. Evaluating conversations as eKGs allows to observe how much knowledge has been accumulated so far, how much diversity of opinions and conflicting information has been encountered, how often the same factoids are mentioned, how long conversations are, and how much knowledge has been acquired per source.

Ratio of mentions to claims Figure 3c shows the ratio of mentions to claims, which relates to how often the same topics are discussed in conversation. An increasing curve implies a repetitive conversation. The blender-Leolani conversation has the steepest curve, as the conversation stagnated with BlenderBot repeating the same factoid ("I have a dog"). In contrast, the Blenderbot-Eliza conversation goes well, almost like the student-Leolani conversations but still repetitive. Once again, the highest quality conversation is the human-human, with the lowest ratio.

Ratio of perspectives to claims Figure 3d shows the ratio of perspectives to claims, where higher means conversations contain more diverse views on the same topics. On the contrary, a lower ratio represents a series of broad conversations on their topics limited to the views of a few, if not only a single source. The lowest curve belongs to

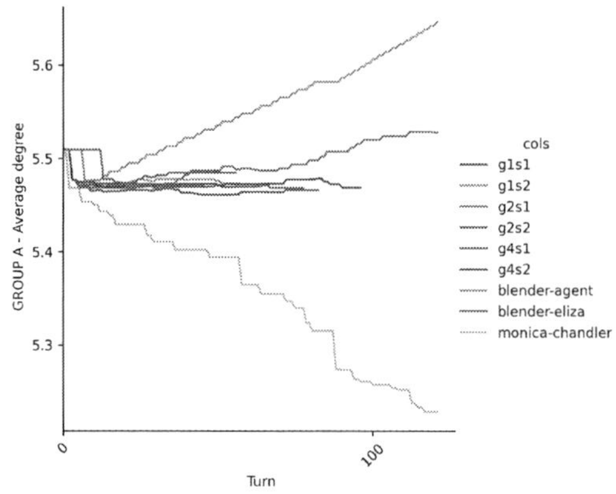

(a) Average node degree.

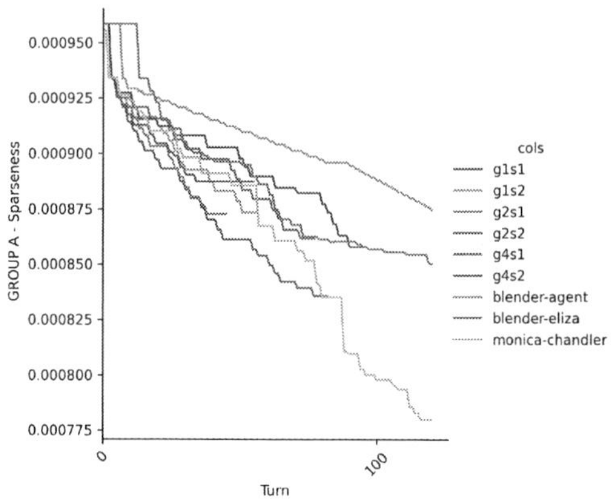

(b) Sparseness.

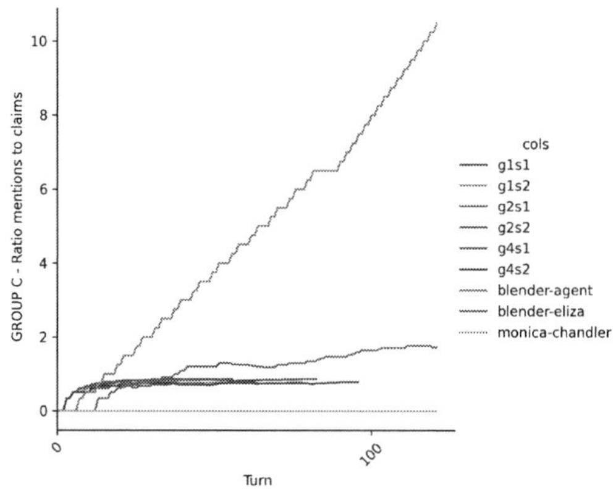

(c) Ratio of mentions to claims.

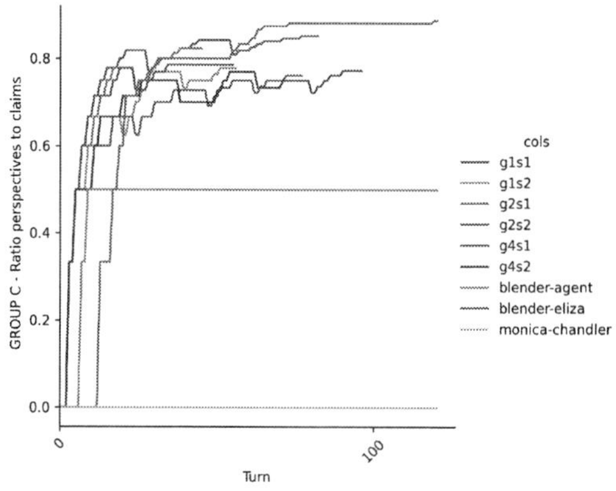

(d) Ratio of perspectives to claims.

Figure 3: Selected graph metrics progression over turns for all student conversations

the Chandler-Monica conversation; due to using StanfordOIE, which does not extract perspectives.

8 Conclusion

We presented a new method for evaluating dyadic interactions that does not require a ground-truth interaction or a human judgment a posteriori. Our method analyses the episodic Knowledge Graph that results from interpreting prompts. Like the USR score, our method is automatic and reference-free. However, we provided evidence that our evaluation correlates better with human judgments and gives deeper insight into the knowledge built up from the conversation. We also conclude that the graph metrics provide nuanced information about the growth of knowledge resulting from the interaction. Although we cannot yet say anything about the absolute score of an interaction, we can compare different interactions based on the resulting graph and observe differences in graph properties that may or may not be desirable.

Note that this line of work aims to approximate human evaluations in a cost-free manner. Yet, human evaluations are generally highly subjective and not reproducible to evaluate a conversation. Thus, even though Overall Human Ratings highly correlate to eKG sparseness, outliers arise due to the impact of individual judgments per student group.

In future work, we want to validate these metrics by evaluating benchmark datasets, similar to the methodology by Li et al. (2019). We also want to direct the conversations to aim for certain types of knowledge and perspectives to validate that our metrics can detect such different intentions. We want to demonstrate that we can associate graph structures with functionality, e.g., having broad or deep knowledge of subjects, being able to direct people to trustworthy informants, or directing people to shared interests.

Supplemental Material Statement: Code and data are publicly available from `https://github.com/selBaez/evaluating-conversations-as-ekg.git`.

Acknowledgements This research was funded by the Vrije Universiteit Amsterdam and the Netherlands Organisation for Scientific Research (NWO) via the *Spinoza* grant (SPI 63-260) awarded to Piek Vossen, the *Hybrid Intelligence Centre* via the Zwaartekracht grant (024.004.022) and the research project (9406.D1.19.005) *Communicating with and Relating to Social Robots: Alice Meets Leolani*.

References

Gabor Angeli, Melvin Jose Johnson Premkumar, and Christopher D Manning. 2015. Leveraging linguistic structure for open domain information extraction. In *Proceedings of the 53rd Annual Meeting of the Association for Computational Linguistics and the 7th International Joint Conference on Natural Language Processing (Volume 1: Long Papers)*, pages 344–354.

Selene Baez Santamaria, Thomas Baier, Taewoon Kim, Lea Krause, Jaap Kruijt, and Piek Vossen. 2021. EMISSOR: A platform for capturing multimodal interactions as episodic memories and interpretations with situated scenario-based ontological references. In *Proceedings of the 1st Workshop on Multimodal Semantic Representations (MMSR)*, pages 56–77, Groningen, Netherlands (Online). Association for Computational Linguistics.

Satanjeev Banerjee and Alon Lavie. 2005. METEOR: An automatic metric for MT evaluation with improved correlation with human judgments. In *Proceedings of the ACL Workshop on Intrinsic and Extrinsic Evaluation Measures for Machine Translation and/or Summarization*, pages 65–72, Ann Arbor, Michigan. Association for Computational Linguistics.

Jan Deriu, Alvaro Rodrigo, Arantxa Otegi, Guillermo Echegoyen, Sophie Rosset, Eneko Agirre, and Mark Cieliebak. 2021. Survey on evaluation methods for dialogue systems. *Artificial Intelligence Review*, 54(1):755–810.

Emily Dinan, Stephen Roller, Kurt Shuster, Angela Fan, Michael Auli, and Jason Weston. 2018. Wizard of wikipedia: Knowledge-powered conversational agents. *arXiv preprint arXiv:1811.01241*.

Siska Fitrianie, Merijn Bruijnes, Deborah Richards, Amal Abdulrahman, and Willem-Paul Brinkman. 2019. What are we measuring anyway? -a literature survey of questionnaires used in studies reported in the intelligent virtual agent conferences. In *Proceedings of the 19th ACM International Conference on Intelligent Virtual Agents*, pages 159–161.

Karthik Gopalakrishnan, Behnam Hedayatnia, Qinglang Chen, Anna Gottardi, Sanjeev Kwatra, Anu Venkatesh, Raefer Gabriel, Dilek Hakkani-Tür, and Amazon Alexa AI. 2019. Topical-chat: Towards knowledge-grounded open-domain conversations. In *INTERSPEECH*, pages 1891–1895.

Chulaka Gunasekara, Seokhwan Kim, Luis Fernando D'Haro, Abhinav Rastogi, Yun-Nung Chen, Mihail Eric, Behnam Hedayatnia, Karthik Gopalakrishnan, Yang Liu, Chao-Wei Huang, et al. 2020. Overview of the ninth dialog system technology challenge: Dstc9. *arXiv preprint arXiv:2011.06486*.

David M. Howcroft, Anya Belz, Miruna-Adriana Clinciu, Dimitra Gkatzia, Sadid A. Hasan, Saad Mahamood, Simon Mille, Emiel van Miltenburg, Sashank Santhanam, and Verena Rieser. 2020. Twenty years of confusion in human evaluation: NLG needs evaluation sheets and standardised definitions. In *Proceedings of the 13th International Conference on Natural Language Generation*, pages 169–182, Dublin, Ireland. Association for Computational Linguistics.

Margaret Li, Jason Weston, and Stephen Roller. 2019. Acute-eval: Improved dialogue evaluation with optimized questions and multi-turn comparisons. *arXiv preprint arXiv:1909.03087*.

Chin-Yew Lin and FJ Och. 2004. Looking for a few good metrics: Rouge and its evaluation. In *Ntcir workshop*.

Yinhan Liu, Myle Ott, Naman Goyal, Jingfei Du, Mandar Joshi, Danqi Chen, Omer Levy, Mike Lewis, Luke Zettlemoyer, and Veselin Stoyanov. 2019. Roberta: A robustly optimized bert pretraining approach. *arXiv preprint arXiv:1907.11692*.

Shikib Mehri and Maxine Eskenazi. Unsupervised evaluation of interactive dialog with dialogpt.

Shikib Mehri and Maxine Eskenazi. 2020. USR: An unsupervised and reference free evaluation metric for dialog generation. In *Proceedings of the 58th Annual Meeting of the Association for Computational Linguistics*, pages 681–707, Online. Association for Computational Linguistics.

Shikib Mehri, Yulan Feng, Carla Gordon, Seyed Hossein Alavi, David Traum, and Maxine Eskenazi. 2022. Interactive evaluation of dialog track at dstc9. pages 5731–-5738.

Kishore Papineni, Salim Roukos, Todd Ward, and Wei-Jing Zhu. 2002. Bleu: a method for automatic evaluation of machine translation. In *Proceedings of the 40th annual meeting of the Association for Computational Linguistics*, pages 311–318.

Romana Pernisch, Daniele Dell'Aglio, Mirko Serbak, and Abraham Bernstein. 2020. Chimp: Visualizing ontology changes and their impact in protégé. In *Fifth International Workshop on Visualization and Interaction for Ontologies and Linked Data*, pages 47–60. CEUR Workshop Proceedings.

Soujanya Poria, Devamanyu Hazarika, Navonil Majumder, Gautam Naik, Erik Cambria, and Rada Mihalcea. 2018. Meld: A multimodal multi-party dataset for emotion recognition in conversations. *arXiv preprint arXiv:1810.02508*.

Hannah Rashkin, Eric Michael Smith, Margaret Li, and Y-Lan Boureau. 2018. Towards empathetic open-domain conversation models: A new benchmark and dataset. *arXiv preprint arXiv:1811.00207*.

Stephen Roller, Emily Dinan, Naman Goyal, Da Ju, Mary Williamson, Yinhan Liu, Jing Xu, Myle Ott, Kurt Shuster, Eric M Smith, et al. 2020. Recipes for building an open-domain chatbot. *arXiv preprint arXiv:2004.13637*.

Yuli Vasiliev. 2020. *Natural Language Processing with Python and SpaCy: A Practical Introduction*. No Starch Press.

Piek Vossen, Selene Baez, Lenka Bajčetić, Suzana Bašić, and Bram Kraaijeveld. 2019. Leolani: A robot that communicates and learns about the shared world. In *ISWC 2019 Satellites*, CEUR Workshop Proceedings, pages 181–184. CEUR-WS. 2019 ISWC Satellite Tracks (Posters and Demonstrations, Industry, and Outrageous Ideas), ISWC 2019-Satellites ; Conference date: 26-10-2019 Through 30-10-2019.

Piek Vossen, Selene Baez, Lenka Bajčetić, and Bram Kraaijeveld. 2018. Leolani: a reference machine with a theory of mind for social communication. In *International conference on text, speech, and dialogue*, pages 15–25. Springer.

Joseph Weizenbaum. 1966. Eliza—a computer program for the study of natural language communication between man and machine. *Communications of the ACM*, 9(1):36–45.

Tianyi Zhang*, Varsha Kishore*, Felix Wu*, Kilian Q. Weinberger, and Yoav Artzi. 2020. Bertscore: Evaluating text generation with bert. In *International Conference on Learning Representations*.

Yizhe Zhang, Siqi Sun, Michel Galley, Yen-Chun Chen, Chris Brockett, Xiang Gao, Jianfeng Gao, Jingjing Liu, and Bill Dolan. 2019. Dialogpt: Large-scale generative pre-training for conversational response generation. *arXiv preprint arXiv:1911.00536*.

A Appendix

A.1 Leolani, the agent

The Leolani agent creates an eKG on the fly and formulates a response to a prompt based on the changes in the graph. At the start, an empty eKG is initialized with the Nice-to-Meet-You (N2MU) ontology (Vossen et al., 2019) that defines basic things in the world such as people, locations, and some social properties, but without any knowledge about individual people. Triple extraction during the conversation adds such knowledge.

In addition to passive processing of human prompts, our agent Leolani reflects on the changing eKG during the conversation. After each change, a series of semantically meaningful SPARQL queries is applied to the eKG to detect specific graph properties that are deemed relevant to respond to. These handmade query patterns detect phenomena like conflicts, uncertainty, analogies, generalizations, knowledge gaps, trust in knowledge sources, the novelty of factoids, and the relevance of factoids to interlocutors. We consider these queries as "*thoughts*" that reflect on the current state of the eKG, given the latest incoming information. Each type of *thought* is associated to a broad higher level goal, which we call "*drives*", for example, to improve the correctness or completeness of the agent's current knowledge, or to improve the engagement or social connection to the interlocutor. These *drives* result in speech acts such as statements or questions that the agent directs to the interlocutor, aiming of obtaining a relevant response. In the next short dialog, the agent Leolani learned a new concept "reading" and tries to generalise this to all people by asking a question to the human. The next statement by the human triggers the agent to ask another follow-up question:

- H: I like reading
- A: I never heard about reading before! can you tell me, is reading something people do?
- H: Yes, people read books
- A: I did not know that, what else do people read?

A.2 Context-Free-Grammar Triple Extractor

Triple extraction is performed by a dependency parser with a Context-Free Grammar (CFG) consisting of 12 rules and a lexicon with mainly closed-class words. It is adapted to resolve deictic references to the addressee or other observed objects in a situation. As the conversation is open and can be about any topic, part-speech-tagging and named entity-recognition is used to detect patterns of open-class words as subjects, predicates, and objects for triples.

A.3 Sample student-Leolani conversations

```
Leolani: "What's up? What is your name?
    Stranger?"

Student1: "Student1"

Leolani: "So your name is Student1?"

Student1: "yes"

Leolani: "Would you like to chat? I'll
    do my best to keep up"

Student1: "I like chatting"

Leolani: "I would like to know. What
    types of Instance like chatting do
    person or Instance usually like"

Student1: "Person likes convos"

Leolani: "I am curious. What types of
    noun or Instance like convos do tops
     or Instance usually like"

Student1: "Convos are not people"

Leolani: "Let me ask you something. Has
    convos work at institution?"

Student1: "I work at institution"

Leolani: "Let me ask you something. Has
    thomas experience touch?"

Student1: "I have experience touch"

Leolani: "I am curious. Has thomas own
    object?"

Student1: "I own object"

Leolani: "Interesting! I am excited to
    get to know about you!"

Student1: "What do you want to know?"

Leolani: "I know agent usually want to
    verb.cognition, but I do not know
    this case"

Student1: "I like sushi"

Leolani: "Exciting news! I did not know
    anything that Student1 like"

Student1: "I also like cats"

Leolani: "If you don't mind me asking.
    What types of animal or Instance
    like cats do person or Instance
    usually like"
```

Listing 1: Extract from conversation with Student 1

A.4 Analysis of student-Leolani conversations

In total, 81,631 triples were generated from the student conversations. Note that not all triples count as factual knowledge. 23 predicates were extracted of which "know" and "be" are most frequent (Table 5). The "know" predicates are mostly derived from introducing oneself to the agent. The predicates further show that the communication is open, although the semantics is not further defined beyond the predicate itself, e.g. there is no relation between "smell" and "can-smell". The triples further contained 31 unique subjects and 78 unique objects; most occurred only once in the communication (Table 6).

Table 5: Predicate labels and their frequency in student conversations.

know	43	can-fly	2	favourite-animal-is	1
be	39	like-to	2	favourite-cat-is	1
like	22	work-at	2	fly	1
live-in	9	be-in	1	hair-color-is	1
sense	7	be-to	1	own	1
have	6	can-learn	1	smell	1
be-from	3	can-smell	1	wear	1
love	3	could-help	1		

Table 6: Entity labels and their frequency in student conversations.

Leolani	23	a-dog	1	go	1
student1	11	a-girl	1	great-that-i	1
student2	10	a-man	1	his-uncle	1
student3	8	a-shame	1	institution	1
student4	8	a-student	1	student10	1
student5	8	a-wise-man	1	know	1
student6	7	a-woman	1	lasagne	1
a-flamingo	6	airplanes	1	phd2-student5	1
student7	6	amstelveen	1	phd2-name	1
student8	5	an-animal	1	Leolani-new-things	1
amsterdam	4	an-aunt	1	my-daughter	1
student9	4	an-emotion	1	my-parents	1
my	3	an-uncle	1	student5-friend	1
orange	3	brown	1	now	1
reading	3	bulgaria	1	object	1
alkmaar	2	business-class	1	other-things	1
cats	2	candy	1	parents	1
chatting	2	city	1	people	1
convos	2	cook	1	person	1
garfield	2	cook-by-myself	1	pink	1
japanese-food	2	deloitte	1	rotterdam	1
love	2	dogs	1	shrimp	1
None	2	every-agent	1	student	1
phd1	2	experience-touch	1	sushi	1
10-fingers	1	favorite-of-student6	1	tapas	1
a-bird	1	flamingo	1	the-south-of-holland	1
a-color	1	food	1	two-hands	1
a-company	1	front-camera	1	what	1
a-country	1	garfield-favourite-food	1	yes-candy	1
a-daughter	1	glasses	1		

A.5 Full list of metrics tested

The full list of 62 metrics used, sorted by group:

- GROUP A
  - Total nodes
  - Total edges
  - Average degree
  - Average degree centrality
  - Average closeness
  - Average betweenness
  - Average degree connectivity
  - Average assortativity
  - Average node connectivity
  - Number of components
  - Number of strong components
  - Shortest path
  - Centrality entropy
  - Closeness entropy
  - Sparseness
- GROUP B
  - Total classes
  - Total properties
  - Total instances
  - Total object properties
  - Total data properties
  - Total equivalent class properties
  - Total subclass properties
  - Total entities
  - Total inverse entities
  - Ratio of inverse relations
  - Property class ratio
  - Average population
  - Class property ratio
  - Attribute richness
  - Inheritance richness
  - Relationship richness
  - Object properties ratio
  - Datatype properties ratio
  - Total concept assertions
  - Total role assertions
  - Total general concept inclusions
  - Total domain axioms
  - Total range axioms
  - Total role inclusions
  - Total axioms
  - Total aBox axioms
  - Total tBox axioms
- GROUP C
  - Total triples
  - Total world instances
  - Total claims
  - Total perspectives
  - Total mentions
  - Total conflicts
  - Total sources
  - Total interactions
  - Total utterances

- Ratio claim to triples
- Ratio perspectives to triples
- Ratio conflict to triples
- Ratio perspectives to claims
- Ratio mentions to claims
- Ratio conflicts to claims
- Average perspectives per claim
- Average mentions per claim
- Average turns per interaction
- Average claims per source
- Average perspectives per source

A.6 Correlation matrix

Hereby we show the full correlation matrix between our proposed metrics and the human and automatic evaluations. Metrics related to conflicts are not informative since the short conversations did not produce conflicting information. Metrics related to perspectives are hindered because the simple triple extractor is limited in the range of perspectives it can extract.

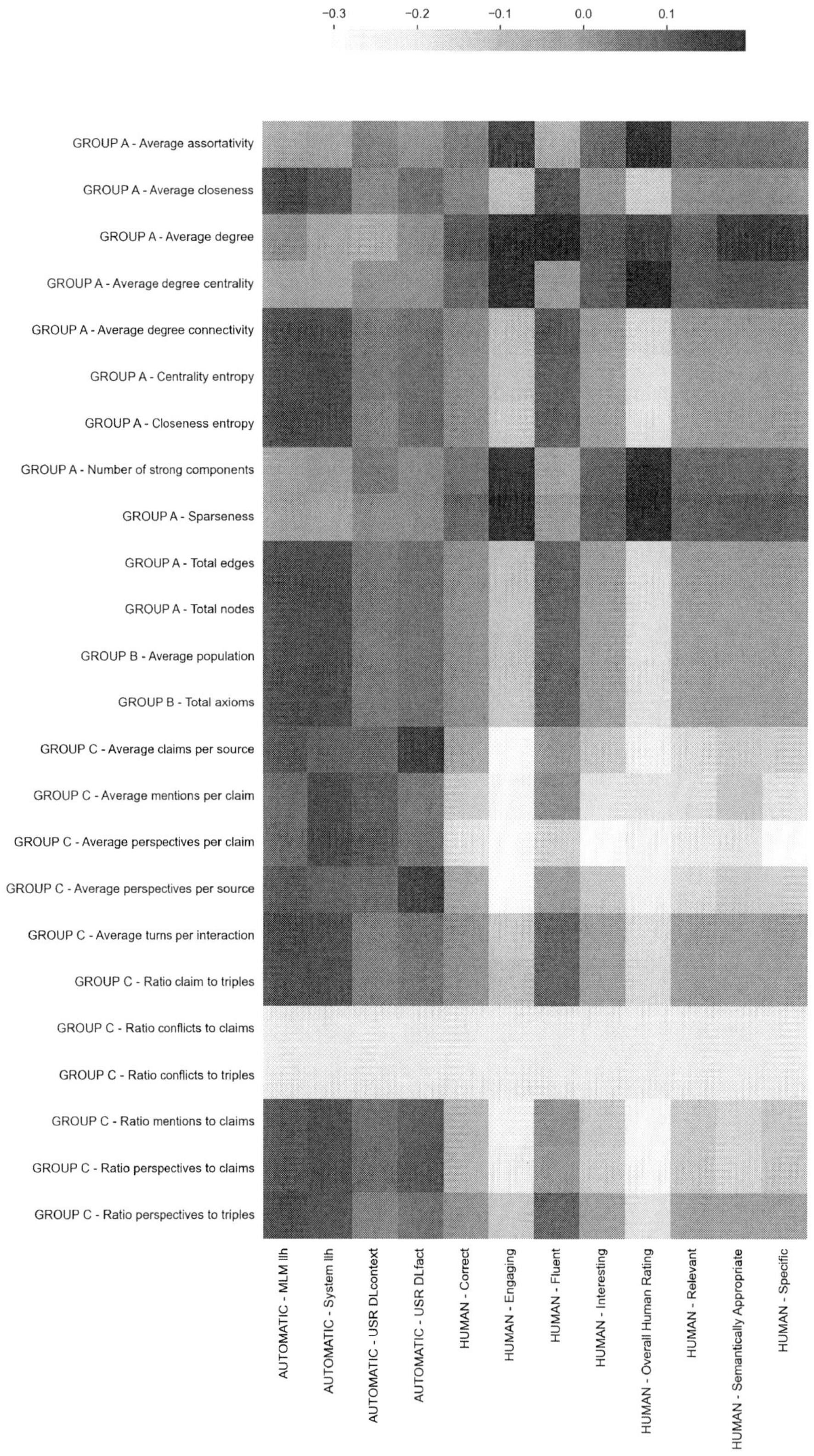

Figure 4: Correlation matrix for evaluation metrics.

PERSONACHATGEN: Generating Personalized Dialogues using GPT-3

Young-Jun Lee[1] **Chae-Gyun Lim**[1] **Yunsu Choi**[2] **Ji-Hui Lm**[2] **Ho-Jin Choi**[1]
[1]School of Computing, KAIST [2]KT Corporation
{yj2961,rayote,hojinc}@kaist.ac.kr {yunsu.choi,jihui.im}@kt.com

Abstract

Recently, many prior works have made their own agents generate more personalized and engaging responses using PERSONACHAT (Zhang et al., 2018). However, since this dataset is frozen in 2018, the dialogue agents trained on this dataset would not know how to interact with a human who loves "*Wandavision.*" One way to alleviate this problem is to create a large-scale dataset. In this work, we introduce the pipeline[1] of creating PERSONACHATGEN, which is comprised of three main components: Creating (1) PROFILEGEN, (2) Persona Set, and (3) PERSONACHATGEN. To encourage GPT-3's generation ability, we also defined a taxonomy of hierarchical persona category derived from social profiling taxonomy (Bilal et al., 2019). To create the speaker consistent persona set, we propose a simple contradiction-based iterative sentence replacement algorithm, named CONL. Moreover, to prevent GPT-3 generating harmful content, we presented two filtering pipelines, one each for PROFILEGEN and PERSONACHATGEN. Through analyzing of PERSONACHATGEN, we showed that GPT-3 can generate personalized dialogue containing diverse persona. Furthermore, we revealed a state-of-the-art Blender 90M trained on our dataset that leads to higher performance.

1 Introduction

Considering users' personal information (e.g., preferences, gender, age, and profession) is an essential capability for chit-chat dialogue agents. Since PERSONACHAT was released in 2018, many studies have attempted to build their own dialogue agents to generate personalized and engaging responses in dialogue. These studies published in ACL Venues usually utilized the PERSONACHAT dataset. However, this dataset was constructed in 2018, so dialogue agents trained on it cannot understand how to interact with users who loved the "*Avengers: End game*" movie, which can be regarded as unseen information. One way to solve this problem is to construct a large-scale dataset that includes more diverse personal information and how to interact with a conversation partner based on them. However, the process of manually creating dataset is time-consuming and costly.

Recently, as an alternate way, many studies have created datasets by leveraging pre-trained language models with designed prompt instructions (Yoo et al., 2021; Baheti et al., 2021; Hartvigsen et al., 2022) due to their enormous ability to produce more human-like text (Clark et al., 2021; Dou et al., 2021). They mainly focused on creating datasets related to NLU tasks, such as text classification, textual similarity, and natural language inference. However, no approach has generated a personalized dialogue dataset using a pre-trained language model, especially GPT-3. Note that our goal is to provide insights that prompting language models can create such datasets, not to release a new dataset generated by a language model.

In this work, we introduce the pipeline of creating PERSONACHATGEN, a small-scale machine-generated dataset of 1,649 dialogues. Motivated by (Mishra et al., 2021) and the collection process of PERSONACHAT, our pipeline consists of three main parts: (1) PROFILEGEN Creation, (2) Persona Set Creation, and (3) PERSONACHATGEN Creation. To obtain high-quality generated results from (1) and (2), we first defined a taxonomy of hierarchical persona category based on the social profiling taxonomy (Bilal et al., 2019). Then, we carefully designed prompts. Since GPT-3 can generate offensive and socially biased text (Baheti et al., 2021; Hartvigsen et al., 2022), we also present filtering steps in our pipeline.

- We introduced a novel pipeline for automatically generating PERSONACHATGEN, that consists of three parts: (1) PROFILEGEN Cre-

[1]Our code is available at https://github.com/passing2961/PersonaChatGen

Proceedings of the 29th International Conference on Computational Linguistic, pages 29–48
October 12–17, 2022.

ation, (2) Persona Set Creation, and (3) PERSONACHATGEN Creation. We can adjust an arbitrary number of dialogue turns, which is a powerful advantage of our proposed pipeline.

- We show that Blender 90M (Roller et al., 2020) trained on PERSONACHATGEN and PERSONACHAT together achieve better performance in both automatic and human evaluation.

- We provide the insight that we can leverage the prompting language model [2] (e.g., GPT-3) to generate personalized dialogues datasets. To the best of our knowledge, this is the first study to automatically generate personalized dialogues using GPT-3.

2 Related Work

Persona Dialogue Generation. Li et al. (2016) encoded persona information into the embedding space. To create more engaging dialogue agents, Zhang et al. (2018) released the PERSONACHAT dataset that was collected from a crowd-sourcing platform (Amazon Mechanical Turk). Madotto et al. (2019) used meta-learning to personalize dialogue agents. Liu et al. (2020) improved the quality of generated responses by incorporating mutual persona perception.

Dataset Generation. Yoo et al. (2021) leveraged GPT-3 to generate datasets for text classification tasks. Schick and Schütze (2021) first released a textual similarity dataset generated using a pretrained language model (PLM) with instructions. Meng et al. (2022) used a unidirectional PLM to generate a dataset that corresponds to given label information for the zero-shot learning of NLU tasks. Then, they fine-tuned a bidirectional PLM using automatically constructed datasets. However, how to generate persona dialogue datasets remain underexplored in the literature.

3 Preliminaries

In this section, we define *persona* and the main terminologies used in this work.

3.1 Task Formulation

This task aims to generate more consistent responses y conditioned on given dialogue context x and persona set P by maximizing $p(y|x, P) = \prod_t p(y_t|y_1, ..., y_{t-1}, x, P)$, where $P = \{p_i\}_{i=1}^N$ and N denotes the number of sentences that the persona set P contains. Since PERSONACHAT (Zhang et al., 2018) is created by two humans who are assigned to each persona set, it contains two persona sets for each dialogue.

3.2 Persona Definition

First, we define a *persona* in this work based on the literature survey. Following the Wikipedia definition [3], a *persona* is simply a fictional character. Li et al. (2016) regarded personas as compositions of identities (background facts or user profile), language behavior, and interaction style. Zhang et al. (2018) defined a persona as a character created by multiple profile sentences. In this work, we define a personas as user profiles. Several works considered each profile sentence (e.g., *I like to play a soccer*) as *personal attribute*, which explicitly represents an identity and characteristics (Welleck et al., 2018; Wu et al., 2019; Wang, 2021). This *personal attribute* is mainly represented in the triple format of (e_1, r, e_2), where e_1, r, and e_2 denote entity 1, relation type, and entity 2, respectively. Herein, we define this relation type as *persona category* and entity 2 as *persona entity*. The *persona entity* is a key-value format. For example, in the *personal attribute* of "*I'm from Boston, MA*", the *persona category* is "location" and the *persona entity* is "(city-state, Boston, MA)".

4 A Taxonomy of Hierarchical Persona Categories

Most previous studies have not explicitly established a taxonomy for the persona category. Welleck et al. (2018) defined various relation types and entity categories (See Appendix F). Furthermore, they presented the hierarchical category for relation types. However, there is significant room to establish more sophisticated categories. We have several reasons for introducing the hierarchical persona category. In the real world, the persona comprises a hierarchical structure. For example, within the "preference" category, there is a preference about "movie" and a further preference about "movie title" or "movie genre." In the practical perspective, we should provide well-designed prompts into GPT-3 to enhance the quality of generated dialogues (Mishra et al., 2021). As we mentioned in

[2] In this work, we use GPT-3 (Brown et al., 2020), but our pipeline could work with any prompting language model, such as OPT (Zhang et al., 2022)

[3] https://en.wikipedia.org/wiki/Persona

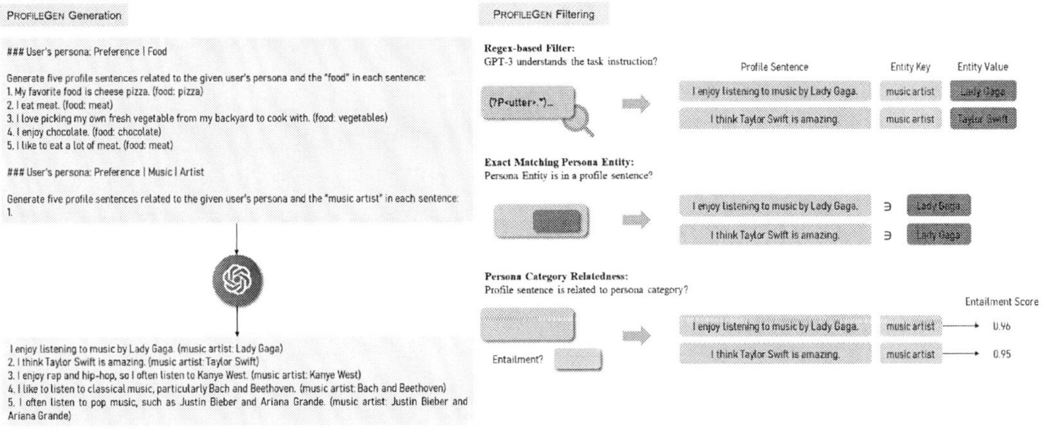

Figure 1: The overall pipeline of PROFILEGEN.

the definition of persona (§3.2), we can regard a persona as a user profile, which can be also viewed as an individual profile. Following (Bilal et al., 2019), we introduce a taxonomy of three main hierarchical persona categories: DEMOGRAPHICS, PSYCHOGRAPHICS, and WELLNESS.

Note that we provide a basic taxonomy of hierarchical persona categories. Appendix E describes these taxonomies in more detail.

5 A Pipeline of Creating PERSONACHATGEN

This section introduces the pipeline of creating PERSONACHATGEN, which consists of three main parts: (i) PROFILEGEN Creation, (ii) Persona Set Creation and (iii) PERSONACHATGEN Creation. To create a consistent persona set, we also propose a simple contradiction-based iterative replacement algorithm, named CONL.

5.1 DECOMPOSITION REFRAMING-based Prompt Engineering

Generating a personalized dialogue dataset from scratch using GPT-3 is challenging for two likely reasons: if a target task itself is inherently difficult or if the task instruction itself is complicated, thus a prompting language model (e.g., GPT-3) cannot achieve higher performance, as reported in Mishra et al. (2021). Furthermore, since the datasets used in GPT-3 pre-training are mainly formal languages (e.g., books and Wikipedia), the generative probability distribution itself learned in GPT-3 will be biased toward formal language. Therefore, we should design prompts to be intuitive and understandable from the GPT-3's perspective.

To make a prompt suitable for creating PERSONACHATGEN, we ponder: "*how was* PERSONACHAT *collected?*" First, they collected 1,155 persona sets. Each persona set P consists of multiple profile sentences (i.e., four or five sentences) and each sentence is written by Turkers. Then, two Turkers chat to get to know one another, where the persona set P is randomly assigned to each Turker.[4] Inspired by this collecting process, we decompose our task into two different sub-tasks, which is similar to the DECOMPOSITION REFRAMING techniques in Mishra et al. (2021). Both creating PROFILEGEN and PERSONACHATGEN parts equally include (1) *generation* describes how GPT-3 generates contents with our designed prompt and (2) *filtering* describes how we remove unreasonable content to enhance the quality of PERSONACHATGEN.

5.2 PROFILEGEN Creation

Here, we describe how we create PROFILEGEN; Figure 1 illustrates the overall process.

5.2.1 Generation

We utilized GPT-3 to create the persona set consisting of multiple profile sentences. In PERSONACHAT, when collecting several profile sentences, the researchers did not explicitly instruct the Turkers to generate sentences corresponding to given *persona categories*. However, in this study, the *persona category* should be explicitly indicated so that GPT-3 understands the given task well. Therefore, we carefully designed the tax-

[4]We omitted the revised personas process, which was originally described in PERSONACHAT (Zhang et al., 2018).

onomy in Section 4. Table 12 and 13 show the prompt template for PROFILEGEN and an example of the constructed prompt with generated profile sentences, respectively.

5.2.2 Filtering

To obtain high quality results, we present a filtering pipeline for PROFILEGEN. Table 1 shows final statistics of filtered results of PROFILEGEN.

Regex-based Filtering. The prompt are providing to GPT-3 has a structured format, which requires generating the *persona category* and *persona entity* in key-value format (shown in Table 12). Thus, we apply the regex pattern to confirm whether it is extracted in the form of a key-value. Otherwise, we can consider that GPT-3 doesn't appropriately understand the given prompt. Appendix J shows our regex pattern.

Exact Matching Persona Entity. We observe that some sentences do not explicitly contain corresponding persona entity keys and values. For example, given the *persona category* "Preference | Music | Artist", GPT-3 generates the sentence *"I love listening to music by Taylor Swift."* with both a *persona entity* key of *"artist"* and a *persona entity* value of *"pop"*. Since this was not an accurate or direct result that we intended, we removed it.

Preserving Persona Category. To verify that GPT-3 generates a profile sentences that are relevant to the given *persona category*, we leveraged an NLI-based zero-shot classification task (Yin et al., 2019), that classifies a sentence through the "entailment" label predicted by NLI model. We used a BART-large (Lewis et al., 2019) model trained on the MNLI dataset (Williams et al., 2017).[5] We removed sentences whose probability values were <90% as predicted by the model. For example, the sentence *"I often listen to Billie Eilish."* is classified as the "music artist" label with 99.7%.

Duplication Filtering. We observe GPT-3 tends to generate repetitive sentences. Thus, we removed duplicated results.

5.3 CONL: Contradiction-based Iterative Sentence Replacement

To create PERSONACHATGEN, we should prepare the persona set, which consists of multiple profile sentences. Unlike PERSONACHAT where each Turker creates a persona set, we should create persona sets automatically by combining the generated profile sentences from above two phases. Hence, we can maintain speaker consistency as if an automatically constructed persona set was written by one speaker. The easiest way is to sample generated sentences randomly. However, this creates inconsistencies between sentences (See Table 11a). To alleviate these inconsistencies, we propose a simple contradiction-based iterative sentence replacement algorithm named CONL; the key idea is that we compare all pairs of sentences within the persona set P.

Specifically, we first prepared sentence pool $\mathcal{M}$ by grouping all profile sentences by persona category. Then, we randomly selected one profile sentence p_i for each persona category and prepared a candidate pool $\mathcal{M}_{cand}$. To calculate the contradiction score between all pairs $\{(p_i, p_j)\}_{i=1,j=2}^{i=50,j=51}$, we leveraged the dialogue contradiction detection (DECODE) task (Nie et al., 2020), which determines whether the previous utterance is inconsistent with any previous utterances. We used a finetuend RoBERTa model (Liu et al., 2019) on the DECODE dataset. [6] Repeatedly getting contradiction scores between p_i and p_j, if a score is higher than the predefined threshold (in this work, we set 0.9 [7]), we replaced the p_j sentence with another sentence by random sampling again from $\mathcal{M}$ corresponding to the persona category. Again, we calculated the contradiction score with all sentences $\{s_i\}$ again. If there were no more s_j sentences to replace, we exclude the entire category from $\mathcal{M}_{cand}$. As such, we create a consistent persona set where all sentences are consistent. In turn, we randomly selected 4-5

	Regex	Exact	Preserving	Dup.
Cumulative Survival Rate (%)	93.76	59.2	47.93	21.78
# of Sentences	69,290	43,753	35,423	16,099

Table 1: The cumulative survival rate of PROFILEGEN for all persona categories after each filtering part. We also describe the number of sentences after each filtering.

[5]https://huggingface.co/facebook/bart-large-mnli

[6]https://huggingface.co/ynie/roberta-large_conv_contradiction_detector_v0

[7]There are two reasons why we set this to 0.9. First, if the threshold is high, we can create a more consistent persona set. Second, our proposed algorithm actually takes a long time. The lower the threshold, the higher the likelihood more sentences will be replaced, which can take a long time. Thus, we judge that it is appropriate to set it to 0.9.

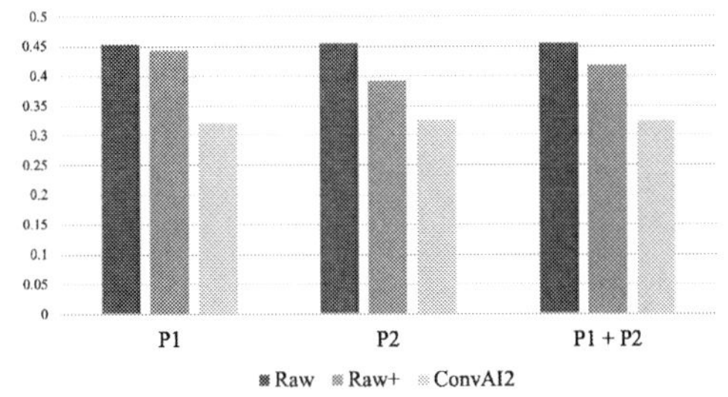

Figure 2: Results of the average F1 score for how many profile sentences are copied to corresponding dialogues.

sentences from the persona set candidate categories pool. However, if five are randomly selected, all sentences might correspond to the DEMOGRAPHICS category. Thus, we simply pull out two sentences that belong to DEMOGRPAHICS, two sentences that belong to PSYCHOGRAPHICS, and one sentence that belongs to WELLNESS. Table 11b shows how CoNL can make a consistent persona set, such as "*I am a very creative and imaginative person.*" and "*I love to read books that are science fiction.*" In a further work, we will apply the speaker detection model (Gu et al., 2021) to create more consistent persona sets.

5.4 PERSONACHATGEN Creation

We describe the overall process of creating PERSONACHATGEN, which is shown in Figure 3.

5.4.1 Generation

If we ask one GPT-3 to create a dialogue while being given two different personas, it can be considered cheating because the model already knows two personas.[8] Therefore, motivated by PERSONACHAT, we use two GPT-3 [9] with two different persona sets created from CoNL (in 5.3). First, we designed our prompt template for generating PERSONACHATGEN based on the prompt provided by OpenAI [10], which we call RAW. However, we observe GPT-3 sometimes simply copies given profile sentences when generating personalized dialogue. We measured how many profile sentences are copied into dialogues by using the F1 scores, which are shown in Figure 2. The average F1 score of RAW is much higher than that of PERSONACHAT because PERSONACHAT asked Turkers not to copy profile sentences into dialogues in explicit instructions. As such, we re-designed RAW prompts by adding the keyword "implicit" (we call it RAW+), which induces it to not produce copies. We show our prompt template for the PERSONACHATGEN and an example of the constructed prompt in Appendix A.1.2.

The advantages of this generation are: (1) GPT-3 doesn't get confused between two different personas, so we expect better-quality dialogues (2) GPT-3 can create by adjusting the number of dialogue turns, which is an impactful advantage due to a recent trend when dealing with long-term memory in dialogues (Xu et al., 2021, 2022).

	Copy-Paste	Consistency	Toxicity.
Cumulative Survival Rate (%)	73.1	46.0	45.3
# of Dialog	2,663	1,675	1,649

Table 2: The cumulative survival rate of PERSONACHATGEN after each filtering part. We also describe the number of dialogues after each filtering.

5.4.2 Filtering

We present a filtering pipeline for PERSONACHATGEN. Table 2 shows final statistics of filtered results for PERSONACHATGEN.

Copy–Paste. Even if we modified RAW, GPT-3 still tends to simply copy the given profile sentences. Since the dialogue generative model trained on this copied dialogues generate dull responses (i.e., simply copying the given persona), we removed dialogues where the number of profile sentences copied is more than one in either persona 1 or 2. We consider it a copied sentence when the F1 score with respect to the utterance is > 0.8.

Persona Consistency. Persona consistency has been a long-standing issue in the dialogue domain. It means that dialogue agents generate utterances that are contradicted in given a subset of its persona. As described in (Brown et al., 2020), GPT-3 can generate repetitive and contradictory sentences. We thought this problem also occurs. To prevent this problem, we leveraged the fine-tuend RoBERTa model on the DECODE dataset which is same model as in §5.3. Specifically, given two persona set

[8]In a toy experiment, we found contradictions and misunderstandings between two given personas as if GPT-3 was confused about the two personas.

[9]Recently, two GPT-3 bots have attempted to discuss human subjects. `https://www.youtube.com/watch?v=jz78fSnBG0s&t=3s`

[10]`https://beta.openai.com/examples/default-chat`

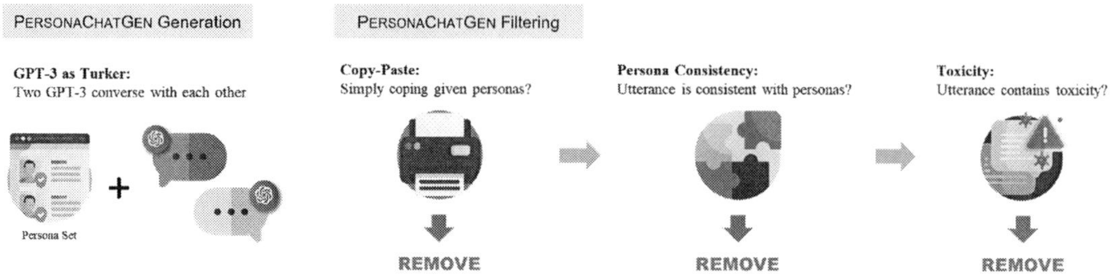

Figure 3: The overall pipeline of PERSONACHATGEN.

Datasets	Source	#Dialog	#Utt.	Avg. #Turns	Avg. Length of Utt.
PERSONACHAT	CS	11k	164k	14.8	14.2
PERSONACHATGEN	GPT-3	1.6k	26k	16.0	9.5

Table 3: Statistics of our PERSONACHATGEN compared to PERSONACHAT which is collected through crowd-sourcing (CS). Utt. indicates utterances.

$P_1 = \{p^1_m\}^5_{m=1}$, $P_2 = \{p^2_m\}^5_{m=1}$ and generated a T length dialogue $C = \{u^1_1, u^2_2, ..., u^1_{T-1}, u^2_T\}$[11], we make a persona–utterance pair (p^1_m, u^1_i) in both P_1 and P_2. We classified these pairs into two labels: contradiction and non-contradiction. If a probability of contradiction label is > 0.9, we regard this pair as having a contradictory relationship. As such, we remove dialogue for which the number of contradictory pairs is more than one in either persona 1 or 2.

Toxicity. Since GPT-3 still produces harmful content such as social bias or offensiveness (Baheti et al., 2021; Hartvigsen et al., 2022), we should remove those that contain such content. To detect toxicity, we use a fine-tuned BERT (Devlin et al., 2018) on the toxic comment classification challenge dataset [12], where this model is provided by the `detoxify` library [13]. We remove any dialogue where the toxicity score of a single utterance is > 0.7.

6 Analysis of PERSONACHATGEN

This section describes the qualitative analysis of PERSONACHATGEN.

[11] In this study, we set $T = 16$.

[12] https://www.kaggle.com/c/jigsaw-toxic-comment-classification-challenge

[13] https://github.com/unitaryai/detoxify

Persona Entity Key	Count		Overlap Ratio(%)
	PERSONACHAT	PERSONACHATGEN	
season	4	13	30.77
music instrument	19	21	25.0
profession	124	116	21.21
animal	54	84	20.0
vehicle	70	82	18.75
food	261	107	13.93
music artist	105	99	8.51
school status	4	97	3.06
book author	7	63	2.94
movie title	1	75	0.0
book title	1	44	0.0

Table 4: Results of the overlapped ratio (%) between entity values of PERSONACHATGEN and PERSONACHAT (Zhang et al., 2018) by measuring the Jaccard similarity. In PERSONACHATGEN, Count denotes the number of entity values corresponding to the entity key.

6.1 Statistics

Table 3 shows the statistics of PERSONACHATGEN. Our PERSONACHATGEN comprises 1,649 dialogues and 26,384 utterances (with roughly 14% the size of PERSONACHAT). Compared to PERSONACHAT, our dataset created by GPT-3 (not a human) had longer utterance lengths and larger utterances included in dialogues. Since our method is based on two GPT-3, we adjusted the number of turns, but this cost too much. In further work, we will reduce the costs by leveraging other available language models at no cost (e.g., OPT (Zhang et al., 2022)).

6.2 Quantitative Analysis

For PROFILEGEN, we measure how much different entity values are generated by GPT-3 by using Jaccard similarity. The lower value indicates more different entities are generated by GPT-3. In Table 4, PROFILEGEN contain more diverse entity values corresponding to *book author*, *movie title*, and *book title*.

	Humanness	Fluency	Category Relevance	Entity Factuality
PROFILEGEN	3.05	3.21	3.46	1.59

(a) Result of PROFILEGEN on humanness, fluency, category relevance, and entity factuality.

	Humanness	Fluency	Relevance	
			P1	P2
PERSONACHATGEN	2.52	2.69	2.39	3.03

(b) Result of PERSONACHATGEN on humanness, fluency, and relevance. P1 and P2 denote two different personas.

Table 5: Human evaluation results of PROFILEGEN and PERSONACHATGEN.

season	0.52	movie genre	0.19
job status	0.48	degree	0.17
place	0.44	family status	0.16
country	0.42	location	0.16
vehicle	0.37	sibling	0.16
marital status	0.34	media genre	0.15
subject	0.33	school status	0.15
personality trait	0.31	age	0.14
music instrument	0.31	show	0.14
profession	0.30	children	0.05

Table 6: Results of inter-rater agreement (Krippendorff's alpha) for each persona entity. We present the degree of agreement as either moderate or fair.

6.3 Qualitative Analysis

We manually checked the quality of both PROFILEGEN and PERSONACHATGEN, where each dataset was conducted on different evaluation metrics except for **Humanness** and **Fluency**. For PROFILEGEN, it is important whether a profile sentence related to a given persona category is created (**Persona Category Relevance**) and whether a generated entity from GPT-3 is accompanied by the given persona category (**Entity Factuality**). For PERSONACHATGEN, it is important whether generated dialogue is consistent for the given persona (**Persona Relevance**). Appendix H contains a detailed description of the evaluation metrics.

For PROFILEGEN, four human annotators evaluated 510 generated sentences (10 sentences for each persona category). In Table 5a, we observe that our PROFILEGEN achieves high performance across all metrics. We measured the inter-rater agreement using Krippendorff's α. Overall, Krippendorff's α is 0.28, which indicates fair agreement. In addition, Table 6 shows the annotator's agreement for each persona entity key.

7 Experiments

To understand how PERSONACHATGEN affects existing the state-of-the-art-model, we trained Blender 90M (Roller et al., 2020) using our dataset.

7.1 Experimental Setting

7.1.1 Datasets

DIALOGUENLI (Welleck et al., 2018) This dataset annotates NLI labels (i.e., entailment, contradiction, and neutral) on PERSONACHAT. For this, they require human annotation of profile sentences and utterances by defining a schema related to relation types (*persona category*) and entity categories (*entity key*). In addition, they present the hierarchy relation types. We lists all information in Appendix F.

PERSONACHAT (Zhang et al., 2018) This dataset was collected through crowdsourcing platform (i.e., Amazon Mechanical Turk) as two Turkers tried to get to know each other based on the personas they were each given. This is a subject of ConvAI2 competition (Dinan et al., 2020) at NeurIPS 2018. In fact, this version was used to fine-tune Blender (Roller et al., 2020).

7.1.2 Persona-based Dialogue Generator

We used Blender (Roller et al., 2020)—a state-of-the-art dialogue generative model—as our generator. We fine-tuned Blender 90M on PERSONACHAT in the same manner as the original paper. For the implementation details, please refer to C.

7.1.3 Evaluation Metrics

To measure the performance of dialogue generative model, we adopted the perplexity (PPL), F1 score, and C score, which are widely used in prior works (Madotto et al., 2019; Kim et al., 2020; Wu et al., 2021). For **PPL** and **F1**, we measured the quality of generated responses by comparing them with the golden response. For **C score**, we measured whether the generated responses are consistent with their given persona by using the fine-tuned BERT-based NLI model from (Kim et al., 2020), which were first introduced in (Madotto et al., 2019).

7.2 Experimental Results

7.2.1 Quantitative Results

Table 7 reports that Blender trained COMB dataset achieves higher performance across all evaluation

P1's Persona	P2's Persona
I have three brothers and sisters. I am the middle child. I'm a big fan of Beyoncé. I like reading books about romance. I have been diagnosed with post-traumatic stress disorder.	I love food and I love to eat. I am a woman who loves fashion. I love reality TV. I prefer to watch comedies. I have hay fever.

Generated Dialogue

P1: Hi, how are you?
P2: I'm good! I love food and I love to eat.
P1: Oh, what's your favorite food?
P2: I love all kinds of food, but my favorite food is probably sushi.
P1: Sushi is really good! I love it too.
P2: Yeah, it's one of my favorite things to eat. I also love fashion.
P1: Beyoncé is a really good fashion icon.
P2: Yeah, she is! I love her style. I also love reality TV.
P1: Oh, what's your favorite reality TV show?
P2: I love a lot of reality TV shows, but my favorite is probably The Bachelor.
P1: The Bachelor is a really good show! I love it too.
P2: Yeah, it's one of my favorite shows. I also love comedies.
P1: What's your favorite comedy?
P2: I love all kinds of comedies, but my favorite is probably The Office.
P1: The Office is a really good comedy! I love it too.
P2: Yeah, it's one of my favorite shows. I also have hay fever.

Figure 4: Example of generated dialogue based on two personas. The teal utterances means directly related to the given P1 and the magenta ones are related to P2.

Model	F1 ↑	PPL ↓	C ↑
[M1] Blender + PERSONACHAT			
PERSONACHAT	18.7	11.30	0.54
COMB	20.3	8.22	0.51
[M2] Blender + COMB			
PERSONACHAT	19.4	11.83	0.63
COMB	24.5	7.79	0.55

Table 7: Results of model performance on the test set of PERSONACHAT and COMB. **[M1]** and **[M2]** refer to Blender 90M finetuned on PERSONACHAT and COMB, respectively. COMB refers to the combination of PERSONACHAT and PERSONACHATGEN.

	Fluency↑	Engagingness↑	Consistency↑
[M1]	3.17	2.53	2.47
[M2]	3.47	2.66	2.69

(a) Results of Human Ratings.

	Win (%)	Lose (%)	Tie (%)
[M2] vs. **[M1]**	47.3	28.7	24.0

(b) Results of Human A/B Test.

Table 8: Human evaluation results comparison for Human Ratings and Human A/B test on 50 samples randomly chosen from the test set of PERSONACHATGEN.

metrics. This implies that PERSONACHATGEN contribute to improve the model performance. Furthermore, we find that Blender trained on PERSONACHAT has relatively lower C score on PERSONACHATGEN compared to one trained on PERSONACHATGEN.

7.2.2 Human Evaluation Results

Following the prior works (Zhang et al., 2018; Kim et al., 2020), we evaluated (i) Human A/B Test and (ii) Human Ratings with three annotators. For Human A/B Test, we asked annotators to choose better responses; they could choose "Tie" if the two given responses are either both good or both bad. For Human Ratings, we asked annotators to rate generated responses on three metrics (using a 4-point Likert scale): **Fluency**, **Engagingness**, and **Consistency**. Appendix H.3 describes the questionnaries and Appendix I system used for the human

P1's Persona	
I'm very short. I have a bird and a fish. I do not know how to play the drums. I like to learn from the books I read, so I tend to gravitate towards non-fiction.	
Dialogue Context	
P2: hey, what's up? P1: Just reading a book. P2: What book?	
Generated Responses	
[M1]	The power of friendship.
[M2]	The catcher in the rye.

P1's Persona	
I am currently employed by google. I am a 20 year old female. I like to play baseball. I like to go hiking in the mountains. I have struggled with crohn's disease for many years.	
Dialogue Context	
P2: hello, how are you? P1: I am good. Just got back from a hike P2: Cool, did you see any animals?	
Generated Responses	
[M1]	No, I'm a bit of a hiker. I like the outdoors.
[M2]	No, I did not see any animals. I just went hiking in the mountains.

Figure 5: Examples of generated responses from **[M1]** and **[M2]** on the test set of PERSONACHATGEN

evaluation.

Table 8 shows that annotators prefer responses generated by Blender trained on PERSONACHATGEN for both Human A/B and Human Ratings. In addition, we measured the inter-rater agreement using Krippendorff's α and obtained 0.12, which implies slight agreement.

7.2.3 Case Studies

As shown in Figure 5, the [M2] model generates more relevant responses to the given persona, which corresponds to the consistency results in Table 8a. In addition, as our PERSONACHATGEN covers diverse persona entities (see in Table 4) compared to PERSONACHAT, the [M2] model generates "*The catcher in the eye*", which is a novel by J.D.Salinger, not "*The power of friendship*", which is a TV series.

8 Conclusion

This paper introduces the pipeline for creating PERSONACHATGEN, a machined-generated dataset of 1,649 dialogues. Our pipeline consists of three main parts: (1) PROFILEGEN creation, (2) Persona Set Creation, and (3) PERSONACHATGEN Creation. Moreover, we present two filtering steps, one for PROFILEGEN and one for PERSONACHATGEN. We reveal that GPT-3 has the ability to generate personalized dialogue datasets on both manual and automatic evaluation. In future work, we intend to leverage OPT (Zhang et al., 2022), which is publicly available and free, with our proposed prompt and pipeline.

Acknowledgements

This work was supported by Institute for Information & communications Technology Planning & Evaluation(IITP) grant funded by the Korea government(MSIT) (No. 2013-2-00131, Development of Knowledge Evolutionary WiseQA Platform Technology for Human Knowledge Augmented Services)

References

Ashutosh Baheti, Maarten Sap, Alan Ritter, and Mark Riedl. 2021. Just say no: Analyzing the stance of neural dialogue generation in offensive contexts. *arXiv preprint arXiv:2108.11830*.

Muhammad Bilal, Abdullah Gani, Muhammad Ikram Ullah Lali, Mohsen Marjani, and Nadia Malik. 2019. Social profiling: A review, taxonomy, and challenges. *Cyberpsychology, Behavior, and Social Networking*, 22(7):433–450.

Tom Brown, Benjamin Mann, Nick Ryder, Melanie Subbiah, Jared D Kaplan, Prafulla Dhariwal, Arvind Neelakantan, Pranav Shyam, Girish Sastry, Amanda Askell, et al. 2020. Language models are few-shot learners. *Advances in neural information processing systems*, 33:1877–1901.

Elizabeth Clark, Tal August, Sofia Serrano, Nikita Haduong, Suchin Gururangan, and Noah A Smith. 2021. All that's' human'is not gold: Evaluating human evaluation of generated text. *arXiv preprint arXiv:2107.00061*.

Jacob Devlin, Ming-Wei Chang, Kenton Lee, and Kristina Toutanova. 2018. Bert: Pre-training of deep bidirectional transformers for language understanding. *arXiv preprint arXiv:1810.04805*.

Emily Dinan, Varvara Logacheva, Valentin Malykh, Alexander Miller, Kurt Shuster, Jack Urbanek, Douwe Kiela, Arthur Szlam, Iulian Serban, Ryan Lowe, et al. 2020. The second conversational intelligence challenge (convai2). In *The NeurIPS'18 Competition*, pages 187–208. Springer.

Yao Dou, Maxwell Forbes, Rik Koncel-Kedziorski, Noah A Smith, and Yejin Choi. 2021. Scarecrow: A framework for scrutinizing machine text. *arXiv preprint arXiv:2107.01294*.

Jia-Chen Gu, Zhen-Hua Ling, Yu Wu, Quan Liu, Zhigang Chen, and Xiaodan Zhu. 2021. Detecting speaker personas from conversational texts. *arXiv preprint arXiv:2109.01330*.

Thomas Hartvigsen, Saadia Gabriel, Hamid Palangi, Maarten Sap, Dipankar Ray, and Ece Kamar. 2022. Toxigen: A large-scale machine-generated dataset for adversarial and implicit hate speech detection. *arXiv preprint arXiv:2203.09509*.

Hyunwoo Kim, Byeongchang Kim, and Gunhee Kim. 2020. Will i sound like me? improving persona consistency in dialogues through pragmatic self-consciousness. *arXiv preprint arXiv:2004.05816*.

Mike Lewis, Yinhan Liu, Naman Goyal, Marjan Ghazvininejad, Abdelrahman Mohamed, Omer Levy, Ves Stoyanov, and Luke Zettlemoyer. 2019. Bart: Denoising sequence-to-sequence pre-training for natural language generation, translation, and comprehension. *arXiv preprint arXiv:1910.13461*.

Jiwei Li, Michel Galley, Chris Brockett, Georgios P Spithourakis, Jianfeng Gao, and Bill Dolan. 2016. A persona-based neural conversation model. *arXiv preprint arXiv:1603.06155*.

Qian Liu, Yihong Chen, Bei Chen, Jian-Guang Lou, Zixuan Chen, Bin Zhou, and Dongmei Zhang. 2020. You impress me: Dialogue generation via mutual persona perception. *arXiv preprint arXiv:2004.05388*.

Yinhan Liu, Myle Ott, Naman Goyal, Jingfei Du, Mandar Joshi, Danqi Chen, Omer Levy, Mike Lewis, Luke Zettlemoyer, and Veselin Stoyanov. 2019. Roberta: A robustly optimized bert pretraining approach. *arXiv preprint arXiv:1907.11692*.

Andrea Madotto, Zhaojiang Lin, Chien-Sheng Wu, and Pascale Fung. 2019. Personalizing dialogue agents via meta-learning. In *Proceedings of the 57th Annual Meeting of the Association for Computational Linguistics*, pages 5454–5459.

Yu Meng, Jiaxin Huang, Yu Zhang, and Jiawei Han. 2022. Generating training data with language models: Towards zero-shot language understanding. *arXiv preprint arXiv:2202.04538*.

Swaroop Mishra, Daniel Khashabi, Chitta Baral, Yejin Choi, and Hannaneh Hajishirzi. 2021. Reframing instructional prompts to gptk's language. *arXiv preprint arXiv:2109.07830*.

Yixin Nie, Mary Williamson, Mohit Bansal, Douwe Kiela, and Jason Weston. 2020. I like fish, especially dolphins: Addressing contradictions in dialogue modeling. *arXiv preprint arXiv:2012.13391*.

Stephen Roller, Emily Dinan, Naman Goyal, Da Ju, Mary Williamson, Yinhan Liu, Jing Xu, Myle Ott, Kurt Shuster, Eric M Smith, et al. 2020. Recipes for building an open-domain chatbot. *arXiv preprint arXiv:2004.13637*.

Timo Schick and Hinrich Schütze. 2021. Generating datasets with pretrained language models. *arXiv preprint arXiv:2104.07540*.

Zhilin Wang. 2021. *Extracting and Inferring Personal Attributes from Dialogue*. University of Washington.

Sean Welleck, Jason Weston, Arthur Szlam, and Kyunghyun Cho. 2018. Dialogue natural language inference. *arXiv preprint arXiv:1811.00671*.

Adina Williams, Nikita Nangia, and Samuel R Bowman. 2017. A broad-coverage challenge corpus for sentence understanding through inference. *arXiv preprint arXiv:1704.05426*.

Chien-Sheng Wu, Andrea Madotto, Zhaojiang Lin, Peng Xu, and Pascale Fung. 2019. Getting to know you: User attribute extraction from dialogues. *arXiv preprint arXiv:1908.04621*.

Yuwei Wu, Xuezhe Ma, and Diyi Yang. 2021. Personalized response generation via generative split memory network. In *Proceedings of the 2021 Conference of the North American Chapter of the Association for Computational Linguistics: Human Language Technologies*, pages 1956–1970.

Jing Xu, Arthur Szlam, and Jason Weston. 2021. Beyond goldfish memory: Long-term open-domain conversation. *arXiv preprint arXiv:2107.07567*.

Xinchao Xu, Zhibin Gou, Wenquan Wu, Zheng-Yu Niu, Hua Wu, Haifeng Wang, and Shihang Wang. 2022. Long time no see! open-domain conversation with long-term persona memory. *arXiv preprint arXiv:2203.05797*.

Wenpeng Yin, Jamaal Hay, and Dan Roth. 2019. Benchmarking zero-shot text classification: Datasets, evaluation and entailment approach. *arXiv preprint arXiv:1909.00161*.

Kang Min Yoo, Dongju Park, Jaewook Kang, Sang-Woo Lee, and Woomyeong Park. 2021. Gpt3mix: Leveraging large-scale language models for text augmentation. *arXiv preprint arXiv:2104.08826*.

Saizheng Zhang, Emily Dinan, Jack Urbanek, Arthur Szlam, Douwe Kiela, and Jason Weston. 2018. Personalizing dialogue agents: I have a dog, do you have pets too? *arXiv preprint arXiv:1801.07243*.

Susan Zhang, Stephen Roller, Naman Goyal, Mikel Artetxe, Moya Chen, Shuohui Chen, Christopher Dewan, Mona Diab, Xian Li, Xi Victoria Lin, et al. 2022. Opt: Open pre-trained transformer language models. *arXiv preprint arXiv:2205.01068*.

A Appendices

A.1 Prompts

In this section, we show our designed prompt template for generating profile sentences and personalized dialogue dataset. All generation processes are based on the one-shot setting. In toy experiment, if we don't provide any in-context examples to GPT-3 (i.e., zero-shot setting), the quality of generated results is not high. Actually, we don't posit an exact reason why zero-shot setting induces degenerated results. The possible reason is that PERSONACHAT task itself is inherently difficult for GPT-3 to understand and follow how to generate corresponded results without in-context examples

A.1.1 Prompts for Creating PROFILEGEN

In Table 12, we show the prompt template (used in §5.2.1) to generate profile sentences. First, we fill out `<Category>`, `<Sub Category>`, and `<Sub Sub Category>` based on the hierarchical persona category (defined in Section 4). Next, we randomly choose five profile sentences with corresponding entity key and value from PERSONACHAT. For example, given in-context examples belonging to "Want | Activity" and target persona category "Preference | Movie | Title", the constructed prompt is presented in Table 13. The profile sentences generated by GPT-3 is marked in blue. We confirm GPT-3 can generate profile sentences with persona entities, which are relevant to the given persona category. It implies that our designed prompt is proper to create profile sentences with various persona entities.

A.1.2 Prompts for Creating PERSONACHATGEN

Table 14 presents the prompt template (used in §5.4.1) to generate PERSONACHATGEN. As we mentioned in §5.4.1, we leverage two GPT-3 as if two humans converse with each other. We construct two prompts including two different personas. Moreover, since we want to encourage GPT-3 to recognize their own persona well, the positions of `You:` and `Friend:` are opposite in two prompts.

B Analysis of PERSONACHATGEN

Table 9 shows full results of the overlapped ratio (%) between entity values of PERSONACHAT and PERSONACHATGEN. Table 10 shows full results of inter-rater agreement for each persona entity.

Persona Entity Key	Count		Overlap Ratio(%)
	PERSONACHAT	PERSONACHATGEN	
season	4	13	30.77
music instrument	19	21	25.0
music genre	52	39	24.66
book genre	28	53	24.62
movie genre	25	42	21.82
profession	124	116	21.21
animal	54	84	20.0
marital status	4	20	20.0
degree subject	41	81	19.61
hobby	122	74	19.51
sport	58	42	19.05
color	43	39	18.84
vehicle	70	82	18.75
age	104	75	17.76
country	25	79	16.85
activity	90	39	16.22
media genre	25	101	15.6
personality trait	196	103	15.0
children	27	61	14.29
food	261	107	13.93
drink	16	67	12.16
workplace	73	81	11.59
gender	3	21	9.09
physical attribute	27	98	8.7
music artist	105	99	8.51
sibling	27	55	7.89
job status	4	37	7.89
city-state	70	56	6.78
family status	27	88	6.48
school type	5	92	5.43
company name	18	22	5.26
subject	41	26	4.69
location	73	141	4.39
eating habit	4	93	4.3
show	25	145	4.29
place	94	99	3.76
school status	4	97	3.06
book author	7	63	2.94
degree	11	97	2.86
school name	20	139	0.63
nationality	25	63	0.0
movie title	1	75	0.0
book title	1	44	0.0

Table 9: Full results of the overlapped ratio (%) between entity values of PERSONACHATGEN and PERSONACHAT (Zhang et al., 2018) by measuring the Jaccard similarity.

C Implementation Details.

To generate PERSONACHAT and PERSONACHATGEN, we leverage an instruct version of GPT-3 (`text-davinci-002`) provided by OpenAI. All experiments are conducted on a single A100 (40GB) GPU. For each stage, the hyperparameter setting used in GPT-3 is as follows:

- For **PROFILEGEN Creation** (§5.2), we set maximum tokens to 128, temperature to 0.7, frequency penalty to 0.4, and presence penalty 0.4. For the stop tokens, we use ###.
- For **PERSONACHATGEN Creation** (§5.4), we set maximum tokens to 128, temperature to 0.8, frequency penalty to 0.4, and presence penalty 0.4. For the stop tokens, we use `You:`, `Friend:`, and `\n`.

season	0.52
job status	0.48
place	0.44
country	0.42
vehicle	0.37
marital status	0.34
subject	0.33
personality trait	0.31
music instrument	0.31
profession	0.3
book genre	0.29
nationality	0.29
degree subject	0.29
food	0.29
book title	0.29
company name	0.29
sport	0.28
drink	0.28
animal	0.28
city-state	0.28
workplace	0.27
hobby	0.26
gender	0.26
school name	0.26
activity	0.26
book author	0.26
music artist	0.26
color	0.25
music genre	0.25
movie title	0.24
physical attribute	0.23
eating habit	0.21
school type	0.21
movie genre	0.19
degree	0.17
family status	0.16
location	0.16
sibling	0.16
media genre	0.15
school status	0.15
age	0.14
show	0.14
children	0.05

Table 10: Full results of inter-rater agreement (Krippendorff's alpha) for each persona entity. We present the degree of agreement as either moderate or fair.

We fine-tuned Blender 90M (Roller et al., 2020) on PERSONACHAT dataset by using default hyperparameter settings provided by a ParlAI framework [14]. Also, we used same hyperparameter settings to fine-tune Blender 90M on COMB for fair comparisons. To compute the persona consistency score (in §5.3 and §5.4.2), we used the finetuned RoBERTa model on the DECODE dataset which achieved 93.71% (reported in (Nie et al., 2020)).

D Persona Set Results

Table 11 shows examples of persona set created by random sampling and CONL.

[14] `https://github.com/facebookresearch/ParlAI`

I am studying at a community college.
I am a teacher at the high school.
"The Great Gatsby" is another book I enjoy.
I'm a big fan of the violin.
I love reading books that are full of adventure.

(a) An example of persona set containing contradiction between profile sentences

I am a very creative and imaginative person.
My older sister is a doctor.
I love to read books that are science fiction
I enjoy watching suspenseful movies.
I have to be very careful in the springtime because of my allergies.

(b) An example of persona set containing no contradiction between profile sentences

Table 11: Examples of persona set created by (a) random sampling and (b) CONL. Red sentences are a case of contradiction.

```
### User's persona: <Category> | <Sub Category> | <Sub Sub Category>

Generate five profile sentences related to the given user's persona and the "<Entity Key>" in each sentence:
1. <Profile Sentence> (<Entity Key>: <Entity Value>)
2. <Profile Sentence> (<Entity Key>: <Entity Value>)
3. <Profile Sentence> (<Entity Key>: <Entity Value>)
4. <Profile Sentence> (<Entity Key>: <Entity Value>)
5. <Profile Sentence> (<Entity Key>: <Entity Value>)

### User's persona: <Category> | <Sub Category> | <Sub Sub Category>

Generate five profile sentences related to the given user's persona and the "<Entity Key>" in each sentence:
1.
```

Table 12: The prompt template which is used for generating PROFILEGEN given the persona category.

```
### User's persona: Want | Activity

Generate five profile sentences related to the given user's persona and the "activity" in each sentence:
1. I have always wanted to travel to ireland or puerto rico. (activity: travel)
2. I hope to visit quebec, canada someday. (activity: travel)
3. One day I would really like to skydive. (activity: skydiving)
4. Before I die, I want to skydive. (activity: skydiving)
5. I hope to see the world with my husband. (activity: travel)

### User's persona: Preference | Movie | Title

Generate five profile sentences related to the given user's persona and the "movie title" in each sentence:
1. I am a big fan of the Lord of the Rings movies. (movie title: Lord of the Rings)
2. I love all of the Harry Potter movies. (movie title: Harry Potter)
3. The Hobbit is one of my favorite movies. (movie title: The Hobbit)
4. I have seen all of the Star Wars movies. (movie title: Star Wars)
5. I enjoy watching Marvel movies. (movie title: Marvel)
```

Table 13: Example of the constructed prompt and generated profile sentences which are marked in blue.

```
### Persona:
<FEWSHOT PERSONA>

The following is a daily conversation with your friend implicitly containing the given persona.
<FEWSHOT CONV>

### Persona:
<TARGET PERSONA>

The following is a daily conversation with your friend implicitly containing the given persona.
You:
```

Table 14: The prompt template which is used for generating PERSONACHATGEN.

E Detailed Information of Taxonomy

E.1 DEMOGRAPHICS

Table 15 shows a taxonomy of DEMOGRAPHICS category with few examples.

Category	Sub Category	Entity Value	Examples	Count
Location	Birthplace	city-state	I was born and raised in the city-state of Detroit, Michigan. I'm from Atlanta, Georgia.	44
		country	I am from Canada. I am originally from Russia.	349
	Residence	city-state	I currently reside in Boston, MA. I currently live in San Francisco, CA.	86
		country	I've also lived in Spain. I moved to Canada when I was five years old.	439
	Nationality	nationality	I'm Italian. I want to be a French citizen.	228
Employment	Company	company name	I would love to work for Google. My company is Facebook.	83
	Workplace	workplace	I am a doctor and I work in a hospital. I am currently employed at a local grocery store.	236
	Profession	profession	I am a salesperson. I am an aspiring writer.	194
	Previous Profession	profession	I was a lawyer, but now I'm retired. I was an accountant for years before I became a stay-at-home mom.	274
	Job Status	job status	I have been employed for 5 years. I quit my job as a waiter.	177
	Teaching Experience	subject	I have a passion for teaching history. I am a teacher and I teach English.	86
		activity	I enjoy teaching people how to cook. I enjoy coaching soccer.	68
School	Status	school status	I am an alumni of the University of Michigan. I graduated from college in May of 2020.	335
	Degree	degree	I am a PhD candidate at XYZ University. I have a master's degree in accounting from harvard.	467
	Degree Subject	degree subject	I have a degree in English from Yale. I am currently getting my PhD in Biology.	489
	Name	school name	I'm in eighth grade at Roosevelt Middle School. I'm currently a sophomore at Yale.	443
	Type	school type	I studied at a public university in the UK. I'm currently attending a four-year university.	434
Family Status	Sibling	sibling	My twin sister and I are very close. My sibling is my best friend.	187
	Children	children	I have two teenage daughters. I am a grandparent with six grandchildren.	119
	-	family status	I am the youngest child in my family. I am a single mother of two teenage daughters.	256
Possession	Animal	animal	I own a panda. I have a dog and I love him	465
	Vehicle	vehicle	I am selling my old car, a bmw. I am the proud owner of a new Tesla.	533
Marital Status	-	marital status	I've been married for 5 years. I am divorced and have been for a few years now.	203
Age	-	age	I just turned 20 last month. I am getting old.	248
Gender	-	gender	I identify as a man. I'm female.	102

Table 15: A taxonomy of DEMOGRAPHICS category. We show few examples per category and blue is the entity value corresponds to given entity key, which is generated by GPT-3. **Count** indicates the final number of profile sentences after our filtering pipelines.

E.2 PSYCHOGRAPHICS

Table 16 shows a taxonomy of PSYCHOGRAPHICS category with few examples.

Category	Sub Category	Sub-Sub Category	Entity Key	Examples	Count
Preference	Food	-	food	I really enjoy mexican cuisine. I love Italian food.	378
	Drink	-	drink	My favorite drink is soda. I always enjoy a cold beer after work.	489
	Animal	-	animal	I'm really interested in reptiles. I once saw a bear in the wild and it was an amazing experience.	671
	Movie	Genre	movie genre	I'm a big fan of sci-fi movies. I prefer watching action movies.	272
		Title	movie title	I have seen all the Harry Potter movies. I'm not a big fan of horror movies, but "A Quiet Place" was really good.	337
	Music	Genre	music genre	I enjoy listening to pop music. I grew up listening to country music and it is still my favorite.	400
		Artist	music artist	On my free time I enjoy listening to Ariana Grande. I prefer rap music, so I often listen to Lil Wayne.	498
		Instrument	music instrument	I like to play acoustic guitar. I am interested in learning how to play the cello.	285
	Book	Author	book author	I love to read books by JRR Tolkien. I also love To Kill a Mockingbird by Harper Lee.	400
		Genre	book genre	I tend to read books from the science fiction genre. I love reading books, but my favorite genre is Romance.	273
		Title	book title	My all-time favorite book is "The Great Gatsby." I prefer The Catcher in the Rye.	352
	Sport	-	sport	I enjoy playing volleyball. I enjoy playing tennis, even though I'm not very good at it.	444
	Location	-	location	My favorite place to go is the park. I love the city.	518
	Media Genre	-	media genre	I prefer to watch dramas. I prefer TV shows that are reality based.	526
	Color	-	color	I love the color white. I enjoy the color pink.	399
	Show	-	show	I used to watch game of thrones, but I got too into it. I also like to watch The Big Bang Theory.	518
	Place	-	place	My favorite place to be is in my garden. I love going to the zoo.	272
	Hobby	-	hobby	I love to play tennis, and I'm pretty good at it too. I like to play video games.	262
	Season	-	season	I love winter because of the Christmas holidays. I love the summer because I can go to the beach.	406
Hobby	Activity	-	activity	-	-
	Sport	-	sport	-	-
	Ability	-	ability	-	-
	Organization	-	organization	-	-
Personal Characteristics	Physical Attribute	-	physical attribute	I prefer men with dark hair. I have brown eyes and dark hair.	239
	Personality Trait	-	personality trait	I am a shy woman. I am a very honest person who always tells the truth.	351
	Eating Habit	-	eating habit	I try to eat healthy. I love to eat vegan food.	224

Table 16: A taxonomy of PSYCHOGRAPHICS category. We show few examples per category and blue is the entity value corresponds to given entity key, which is generated by GPT-3. **Count** indicates the final number of profile sentences after our filtering pipelines.

Category	Sub Category	Entity Key	Examples	Count
Disease	Respiratory	respiratory disease	I have emphysema and get out of breath easily. I was diagnosed with bronchitis a few weeks ago and I'm still recovering.	318
	Digestive	digestive disease	I was diagnosed with Crohn's disease when I was eighteen. I have celiac disease.	232
Symptom	Physical	physical symptom	I start sneezing when I eat peanuts. I have a lot of stomach problems because I eat junk food all the time.	267
	Psychiatric	psychiatric symptom	I have OCD and panic attacks. I have PTSD.	267

Table 17: A taxonomy of WELLNESS category. We show few examples per category and blue is the entity value corresponds to given entity key, which is generated by GPT-3. **Count** indicates the final number of profile sentences after our filtering pipelines.

E.3 WELLNESS

Table 17 shows a taxonomy of WELLNESS category with few examples.

F Schema in DIALOGUENLI

F.1 Hierarchy Relation Types

Location, Employment, School, Likes, Hobbies, Wants, Favorites, Possessions, Personal

F.2 Relation Types

place_origin, live_in_citystatecountry, live_in_general, nationality, employed_by_company, employed_by_general, has_profession, previous_profession, job_status, teach, school_status, has_degree, attend_school, like_general, like_food, like_drink, like_animal, like_movie, like_music, like_read, like_sports, like_watching, like_activity, like_goto, dislike, has_hobby, has_ability, member_of, want_do, want_job, want, favorite_food, favorite_color, favorite_book, favorite_movie, favorite_music, favorite_music_artist, favorite_activity, favorite_drink, favorite_show, favorite_place, favorite_hobby, favorite_season, favorite_animal, favorite_sport, favorite, own, have, have_pet, have_sibling, have_chidren, have_family, have_vehicle, physical_attribute, misc_attribute, has_age, marital_status, gender, other

F.3 Entity Categories

ability, activity, animal, color, citystate, country, company, cuisine, degree_type, drink, family, food, gender, general_location, job_status, language, marital, media_genres, media_other, movie_title, music_artist, music_genre, music_instrument, noun, number, organization, person, person_attribute, person_label, personality_trait, profession, read_author, read_genre, read_title, read_other, school_name, school_status, school_type, season, sport_type, subject, time, vehicle, location, other

G More Examples of PERSONACHATGEN

Figure 6 shows more examples of PERSONACHATGEN. Overall, generated dialogues are natural and consistent with the given personas.

P1's Persona	**P2's Persona**
I love food and I love to eat. I am a woman who loves fashion. I love reality TV. I prefer to watch comedies. I have hay fever.	I've been to Italy three times. I graduated from Yale. I've read all of the books by Jodi Picoult. I'm a big fan of books, and my favorite genre is fantasy. I have asthma and it makes it hard to breathe sometimes.

Generated Dialogue

P1: Hey, how are you?
P2: I'm good, just got back from Italy.
P1: Oh, how was it?
P2: It was great, I love it there.
P1: What did you eat?
P2: Everything, I love Italian food.
P1: That sounds amazing, I need to go there sometime.
P2: Yeah, you should definitely go. It's a great place.
P1: I also love fashion, do you follow any trend?
P2: No, not really. I prefer classic styles.
P1: That's cool, I like to watch reality TV.
P2: Yeah, I don't really watch much TV. I prefer to read.
P1: That's great, what do you like to read?
P2: I like to read books, my favorite genre is fantasy.
P1: That's great, I have hay fever so I can't really read outside.
P2: Yeah, I have asthma so it's hard for me to breathe sometimes.

P1's Persona	**P2's Persona**
I am retired from my previous job as a software engineer. I do not travel. I like to learn from the books I read, so I tend to gravitate towards non-fiction. I also enjoy watching movies.	He is a transgender man. I am very responsible. I like to watch action movies because they're exciting and fun. When I'm feeling down, I always listen to Sam Smith to cheer me up.

Generated Dialogue

P1: Hi, how are you today?
P2: I'm good, how are you?
P1: I'm good, thanks for asking. What have you been up to lately?
P2: Just hanging out with friends and family. What about you?
P1: I've been reading a lot of books lately.
P2: That sounds really great. What kind of books?
P1: Mostly non-fiction. I like to learn from the books I read.
P2: That's really admirable. I need to start reading more books.
P1: Yes, I think it's really beneficial. Do you like watching movies?
P2: Yeah, I love watching movies. Action movies are my favorite.
P1: That sounds great. I enjoy watching movies too.
P2: What's your favorite movie?
P1: I don't really have a favorite movie. I just enjoy watching movies in general.
P2: That's a great attitude to have.
P1: Thanks. I think it's important to just enjoy the experience and not worry about picking a favorite.
P2: That's definitely a good way to look at it.

Figure 6: Examples of generated dialogue based on two personas. The teal utterances means directly related to the given P1 and the magenta ones are related to P2.

H Human Evaluation Questionnaire

We present a list of questions and multiple-choice options used for human evaluation for PROFILEGEN and PERSONACHATGEN.

H.1 PROFILEGEN

- HUMANNESS: Do you think this conversation is from a model or a human?

  Options: 1: Definitely a model / 2: Probably a model / 3: Probably a human / 4: Definitely a human

- FLUENCY: Does this conversation seem contextually natural? Could you understand this conversation?

  Options: 1: Very unnatural / 2: Mostly unnatural / 3: Mostly natural / 4: Very natural

- PERSONA CATEGORY RELEVANCE: How consistent this sentence is with respect to the given persona category

  Options: 1: Not at all / 2: A little / 3: Somewhat / 4: A lot

- ENTITY FACTUALITY: Does this entity is accompanied by the given persona category?

  Options: 0: No / 1: Don't know / 2: Yes

H.2 PERSONACHATGEN

- HUMANNESS: Do you think this conversation is from a model or a human?

  Options: 1: Definitely a model / 2: Probably a model / 3: Probably a human / 4: Definitely a human

- FLUENCY: Does this conversation seem contextually natural? Could you understand this conversation?

  Options: 1: Very unnatural / 2: Mostly unnatural / 3: Mostly natural / 4: Very natural

- PERSONA RELEVANCE: How consistent this conversation is with respect to the given persona (i.e., given profile sentences)

  Options: 1: Not at all / 2: A little / 3: Somewhat / 4: A lot

H.3 For Human Ratings

- CONSISTENCY: How much consistent did this user speak with respect to the given persona?

  Options: 1: Not at all / 2: A little / 3: Somewhat / 4: A lot

- ENGAGINGNESS: How much did you enjoy talking to this user?

  Options: 1: Not at all / 2: A little / 3: Somewhat / 4: A lot

- FLUENCY: How naturally did this user speak English?

  Options: 1: Very unnatural / 2: Mostly unnatural / 3: Mostly natural / 4: Very natural

I Human Evaluation System

Here is a screenshot of human evaluation system. Based on Python Flask APIs and a Web user interface with Javascript, we implemented an annotation tool for scoring the generated results from our conversational model. Each annotator can read each conversation's persona descriptions and dialog sentences and choose their scores according to human evaluation metrics such as fluency. All changes are immediately stored on the server-side database by accessing the Flask APIs.

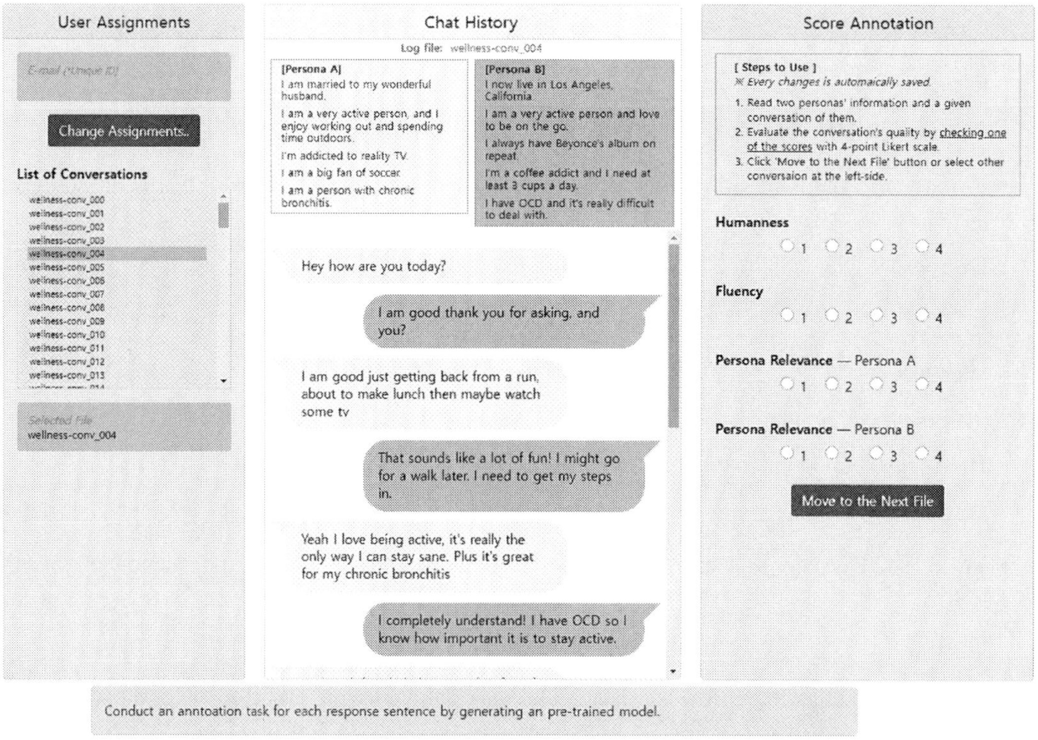

Figure 7: Screenshot of the human evaluation system for manually checking overall quality of generated personalized dialogues.

J Regex Pattern

Since GPT-3 sometimes generates the key-value information with the square brackets [] not the parenthesis (), we consider the square brackets in the regex pattern. Finally, for the regex-based filtering (in §5.2.2), we use the following pattern:

```
(?P<utter>.*)[\(|\[](?P<attr>.*): (?P<value>.*)[\)|\]]
```

Author Index